PUMPED

The Boston Globe

This book is available in quantity at special discounts for your group or organization. For further information, contact:

Triumph Books LLC
814 North Franklin Street
Chicago, Illinois 60610
www.triumphbooks.com
@TriumphBooks

Printed in U.S.A.
ISBN: 978-1-62937-059-0

TRIUMPHBOOKS**.COM**

BOOK STAFF
EDITOR Janice Page
ASSISTANT EDITOR/WRITER Ron Driscoll
ART DIRECTOR Rena Anderson Sokolow
DESIGNER Cynthia Daniels
RESEARCHERS/PROOFREADERS Kevin Coughlin, James Page, William Herzog, Richard Kassirer

PHOTOGRAPHERS
THE BOSTON GLOBE Barry Chin, 22, 24, 55, 58, 60, 69, 71, 87, 97, 107 • Jim Davis, 7, 12, 14, 18, 21-23, 23, 26, 46, 73, 77-81, 85, 89, 99, 104-106, 110, 123 • Stan Grossfeld, 40, 44, 108 • Robert E. Klein, 117 • Matthew J. Lee, 32, 41, 42, 83, 91-95, 113 • Frank O'Brien, 102 • David L. Ryan, 45 • Jonathan Wiggs, 115 • file, 103.

ADDITIONAL PHOTOS COURTESY OF
AP/Wide World Photos, 75 (Charlie Riedel) • 53 (Charles Krupa) • 119 (Mark Humphrey) • 28 (Matt Rourke) • 31 (Matt Slocum).
Getty Images, 5 (Rob Carr) • 15 (Kevin C. Cox) • 36 (Mike Lawrie) • 2, 20, back cover (Tom Pennington) • front cover, 1, 16, 128 (Christian Petersen) • 121 (Joe Robbins) • 38, 62 (Jim Rogash) • 126 (Jamie Squire) • 54 (Jared Wickerham) • 59 (file).

With special thanks to Boston Globe publisher John W. Henry, chief executive officer Mike Sheehan, and editor Brian McGrory • Joe Sullivan and the Boston Globe sports department • Bill Greene and the Globe photo department • Lisa Tuite and the Globe library staff • Mary Zanor, John Gates, and Elevate Communications • Mitch Rogatz, Kristine Anstrats, and the team at Triumph Books • Chris Jackson and Quad/Graphics of Taunton • Todd Shuster, Lane Zachary, and Zachary Shuster Harmsworth Literary Agency.

Front cover New England Patriots quarterback Tom Brady won his fourth Super Bowl and his third Most Valuable Player award in stunning fashion.

Opposite page Patriots owner Robert Kraft had a tight grip on the Lombardi Trophy after his team defeated the Seattle Seahawks in Super Bowl XLIX at the University of Phoenix Stadium.

Back cover A decade after their last Super Bowl triumph, which followed the 2004 season, quarterback Tom Brady (left), owner Robert Kraft, and head coach Bill Belichick celebrated Super Bowl Trophy No. 4.

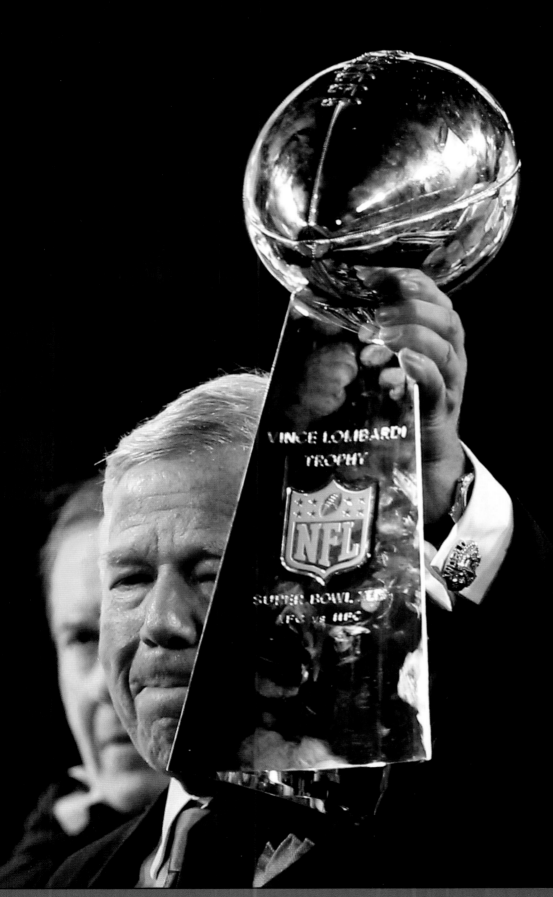

CONTENTS

INTRODUCTION

BY JOHN POWERS / Globe Staff

The air had gone out of the season before the leaves turned, when the Patriots were flattened 41-14 at Kansas City. "Can they turn it around?" Tedy Bruschi, who had won three rings wearing red, white and blue, mused during his ESPN weekly chat. "I think it's going to be hard. Very hard." » Of all New England's championships, this was the most arduous to achieve, yet one of the most fulfilling. The team trailed in 11 of its 16 regular-season games and twice had to come from two touchdowns behind to beat Baltimore in their divisional duel. Its coach and quarterback were accused of deception and deflation. Yet the Patriots found redemption in the same Arizona desert where perfection went pffffft! seven years ago. » "We're bringing this thing back to Foxborough," crowed receiver Julian Edelman, who caught the winning touchdown, then cradled the Lombardi Trophy as New England won, lost and then won its fourth Super Bowl crown in the final two minutes, taking down defending champion Seattle 28-24 with the populace of 44 states rooting against the Brady Bunch. "It feels unbelievable." » After the Patriots lost their last two title shots to the Giants, Bill Belichick finally equaled Chuck Noll for most Super Bowl victories by a head coach, and Tom Brady drew even with boyhood idol Joe Montana and Terry Bradshaw for most by a quarterback. But nobody figured that the play of the season would be made by an undrafted rookie in the final moments. "I just had a vision I was going to make a big play and it came through," said Malcolm Butler, who picked off a pass that nobody but he thought that the Seahawks would throw from the 1-yard line. » It was the most unlikely climax in Super Bowl history and it capped a most extraordinary season. The Patriots made it back to the championship game with a mix-and-match offensive line, revolving running backs, a rebuilt secondary and a few unknowns who had the Foxborough faithful scratching their heads. Tim Wright? Brian Tyms? Jonas Gray? Butler? Yet they found a way to win a sixth straight AFC East title, then grounded the Ravens and corralled the Colts. "I only have one thing to say: We're on to Seattle," Belichick declared after his club had advanced to the championship bout for a record sixth time in 14 years.

Nobody was predicting that in September when the Chiefs, who didn't even make the playoffs, manhandled New England on Monday Night Football. But New England survived that prime-time pounding by resorting to instant amnesia. "We're on to Cincinnati," Belichick kept insisting.

The subsequent 43-17 decision over the unbeaten Bengals proved an ideal restorative. After that the Patriots lost only twice – at Green Bay and in the regular-season finale with Buffalo, which they treated as an exhibition outing.

Not that it was easy. New England twice needed to block field goals to hold off the Jets. And getting past Baltimore, which had twice snatched away Super Bowl tickets, required a bit of legal trickery. Edelman, the receiver who hadn't thrown a pass since he was a Kent State quarterback, hooked up with Danny Amendola on a 51-yard touchdown strike off a lateral from Brady. And New England's shell-game switching of eligible and ineligible receivers had the Ravens defenders befuddled. "Maybe those guys gotta study the rule book and figure it out," mused Brady after rival coach John Harbaugh complained to officials.

The Patriots didn't need any chicanery in their 45-7 runaway over Indianapolis. "They could have played with soap for balls and beat us," tweeted Colts tight end Dwayne Allen. But when all but one of New England's game balls was reported to be at least a pound light at halftime, "Deflategate" became a national obsession, with everyone from Hall of Fame quarterbacks to MIT physicists weighing in.

The Patriots, who have traditionally thrived on Us Against the World motivation, were determined to settle all arguments at the Super Bowl. "It wasn't the way we drew it up," conceded Brady, who threw four touchdown passes en route to his third MVP trophy. "We never doubted each other."

Patriot players, including Tom Brady (12) and Nate Ebner (43), charge onto the field before the big game.

XL

SUPER BOWL

'NUMBER ONE: DO YOUR JOB. NUMBER TWO: PUT THE TEAM FIRST.'

BILL BELICHICK · PATRIOTS COACH

BY CHRISTOPHER L. GASPER / Globe Staff

Tom Brady grew up in San Mateo, Calif., looking up to San Francisco 49ers great Joe Montana. After Super Bowl XLIX, Brady can now look him square in the eye and ask him to compare ring collections. It's all even because Brady conducted the largest fourth-quarter comeback in Super Bowl history, rallying his team from a 10-point deficit to a pulsating 28-24 victory over the Seattle Seahawks at University of Phoenix Stadium. » The 70,288 in attendance and billions more watching on television bore witness to Brady taking a jack to his historical pedestal and cranking it up a few notches by winning his fourth Super Bowl, joining Montana and Pittsburgh Steelers great Terry Bradshaw on the Super Bowl summit. » This was the essence of Brady's career — beating the odds, refusing to quit, staying calm under pressure, and delivering when it mattered most. The 37-year-old quarterback everyone said was in decline after a disastrous Monday night in Kansas City in September lifted the Patriots back to the top of the football »20

0

Career receptions entering the Super Bowl for Seattle's Chris Matthews, who had 4 catches for 109 yards and a touchdown in the game.

2

Interceptions thrown by Tom Brady against the Seahawks. He had a total of two interceptions in his five previous Super Bowl games, against nine touchdowns.

4

Super Bowl victories for New England coach Bill Belichick, which ties him with Pittsburgh Steelers coach Chuck Noll for the most ever.

4.3

Average yards per rush for Seattle's Marshawn Lynch, who ran for 102 yards on 24 carries in the game with a touchdown.

10

Points the Patriots trailed by in the fourth quarter,
the largest deficit a team has ever overcome in the second
half of a Super Bowl.

10

Years between Super Bowl victories for Tom Brady,
whose last win came in 2005 vs. Philadelphia, the longest
span between wins for a Super Bowl QB..

0:29

Seconds it took the Seahawks to go 80 yards in
five plays for the tying touchdown at the end of the first
half, helped by a 15-yard penalty vs. the Patriots.

37

Completions by Tom Brady vs. the Seahawks, which
broke the Super Bowl record of 34, set in 2014 by Peyton
Manning in the Broncos' loss to Seattle.

Patriots wide receiver Brandon LaFell (19) shakes free from Seattle safety Earl Thomas III to score the game's first touchdown on an 11-yard pass from Tom Brady.

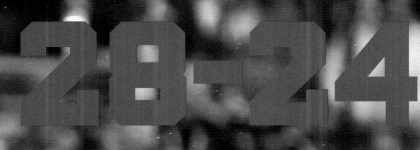

28-24

NE	0	14	0	14
SEA	0	14	10	0

Rob Gronkowski (87) snares a 22-yard, second-quarter touchdown throw from Tom Brady to put the Patriots up, 14-7. Danny Amendola (80) gathers in a 4-yard toss at the back of the end zone in front of Seattle safety Earl Thomas III in the fourth quarter to bring the Patriots within three points at 24-21.

Tom Brady celebrates after connecting on a second-quarter touchdown pass, one of four TD throws for Brady in the game, which gave him a Super Bowl-record 13 career touchdown passes.

Julian Edelman hauls
in a third-quarter pass
from Tom Brady, one
of nine catches for
Edelman in the game,
which accounted for 109
yards and one Patriot
touchdown.

»FROM 9 • world in February, one pass at a time.

No one has won more with less or done it more consistently than TB12, who dropped the boom on the Seahawks' Legion of Boom secondary in the fourth quarter, going 13 of 15 for 124 yards and two touchdowns. His 50th and final toss of the night was a 3-yard pass to Julian Edelman with 2:02 left that put the Patriots up for good and gave him a Super Bowl career-record 13 TD passes.

Finally armed with a defense that could close the deal, Brady captured his first Super Bowl in 10 seasons and won his third Super Bowl MVP award, tying Montana.

It had been a tough week for Brady. He had a cold. He was dogged by the allegations that he had something to do with the deflated footballs the Patriots played with in the AFC Championship game against the Colts. Even his idol, Montana, pointed the finger at Brady in Deflategate.

The only thing Brady deflated in Super Bowl XLIX was the hopes of the Seahawks, who had humbled Brady's QB contemporary, Peyton Manning, last year in the Super Bowl.

It was clear from the beginning that the Patriots were winning

or losing this game on Brady's gilded right arm, and he finished with a Super Bowl-record 37 completions for 328 yards and four touchdowns with two interceptions.

The comeback Brady led was in part his own creation.

He threw two interceptions, one in the Seattle end zone in the first quarter. The other led to a Russell Wilson-to-Doug Baldwin touchdown toss that gave the Seahawks and their boisterous 12th Man backers a 10-point lead.

"I never feel I'm out of the game with Tom," said Brandon LaFell, who caught one of Brady's four TD passes. "If we're down, 7 or 14 or whatever, we're two plays from being back in the game at any time. With Tom with the ball in his hands we've always got a chance."

Saint Thomas of San Mateo led the Patriots on a nine-play, 68-yard march to pull within 3, capping it with a 4-yard touchdown toss to Danny Amendola.

After the Patriots forced a three-and-out, Brady took the Patriots 64 yards in 10 plays, completing all eight of his passes for the win.

This was the third time in the Patriots' last three Super Bowl appearances that Brady had left

the field late with the lead.

Both of the previous times against the Giants, in Super Bowl XLII and Super Bowl XLVI, he ended up back on the field, chasing victory. It looked like it could be headed that way again when Seattle got an improbable catch from wide receiver Jermaine Kearse that gave the Seahawks first and goal at the 5.

But inexplicably Seattle eschewed using human battering ram Marshawn Lynch and called a pass on second and goal from the 1. It was intercepted on a slant pass by undrafted rookie Malcolm Butler, a player as far from Brady on the spectrum of the Patriots' roster as possible.

Brady isn't the Greatest of All Time today without Butler's play, just like David Tyree's miracle catch in '08 has nothing to do with Brady's personal oeuvre.

He knows that.

"I never put myself in those discussions," Brady said. "That's not how I think. There are so many great players that have been on so many great teams, and we've had some great teams that haven't won it. I think you just enjoy the moment."

In this moment or any other, there is no quarterback who has ever played the game better than Thomas Edward Patrick Brady.

Tom Brady and Vince Wilfork – the only two Patriots remaining from their 2004 championship team – celebrate again.

THE GATEKEEPERS

Vince Wilfork was on the field when the Patriots defense let the Giants drive for the game-winning touchdown in the Super Bowl seven years ago. He was on the field again three years ago when New England's defense again couldn't stop Eli Manning from leading the Giants for the game-winning score in the final minutes.

This time, Wilfork and the defense finally got their redemption.

"To be a defensive player, to be on the field and put a stamp on it for us, that's the most amazing feeling right now," said Wilfork. "All year, we talked as a defense that we wanted to make plays when it counted. We wanted our teammates to count on us."

And they delivered.

The Patriots managed to keep Seattle off the scoreboard for the final 19:54 of the game. After the Seahawks took a 24-14 lead, they gained just one first down on their next three possessions and punted all three times.

But the key play — the one Patriots fans will tell their grandkids about — was rookie Malcolm Butler's interception in the end zone on second and goal from the 1 with 26 seconds left in the game.

"He just went down in history," safety Patrick Chung said.

Seahawks coach Pete Carroll will be second-guessed for eternity for calling a pass on second down from the 1-yard line, especially with Marshawn Lynch (104 yards, 1 TD) running so well.

"I think everybody was expecting run," linebacker Dont'a Hightower said.

Everyone except Carroll and Butler, that is. Carroll said that he didn't like the matchup against New England's goal-line package. Carroll viewed second and 1 as almost a throw-away play.

Credit Butler and the Patriots for doing their homework. They noticed the Seahawks came out in their three-receiver set, with Jermaine Kearse and Ricardo Lockette stacked on the right.

"In preparation I remembered the formation they were in — two-receiver stack. I just knew they were running a pick route," Butler said.

Sure enough, Kearse ran a clear-out, and Lockette tried to run a quick slant underneath him. But Butler jumped the play perfectly and beat Lockette to the football, hauling in the interception and holding on for dear life. It was the first NFL interception for Butler, an undrafted rookie.

"Goal line, three cornerbacks, you know they're going to throw it," Butler said. "I had a feeling I was going to make a big play, but not that big."

Just two plays before his interception, Butler allowed a 33-yard pass to Kearse that he tipped in the air, was bobbled several times, and miraculously fell into Kearse's lap. This was David Tyree, all over again – before Butler flipped the script.

"We call him 'Scrap,' because the first time we saw him, he was just so scrappy, around the ball the whole time," Wilfork said of Butler. "That moment with him making that play, it's just a fairytale end to the book because of what he's done all year for us."

BEN VOLIN • *Globe Staff*

Patriots All-Pro special teams player Matthew Slater rejoices.

'MY MOM SAID SHE STOPPED WATCHING IN THE LAST TWO MINUTES AND JUST PRAYED.'
DEVIN MCCOURTY · PATRIOTS SAFETY

'TO WIN THE SUPER BOWL BY A DEFENSIVE STOP, I'M TELLING YOU, IT'S PRICELESS.'
VINCE WILFORK · PATRIOTS DT

Seahawks wide receiver Jermaine Kearse (15) makes an incredible juggling catch for a 33-yard gain against the Patriots Malcolm Butler (21) with 1:06 to play to set the Seahawks up at the Patriot 5-yard line.

Patriots rookie cornerback Malcolm Butler (21) outduels Seattle's Ricardo Lockette (83) to make a goal-line interception of Russell Wilson's pass with 20 seconds to play in the game.

Malcolm Butler (right, without helmet) is stunned as he leaves the field with his teammates after making the game-saving play for the Patriots in the final minute.

Seahawks coach Pete Carroll, center, watches his players return to the bench after Russell Wilson threw an interception from one yard out with 20 seconds to play. Carroll later said, "The guy [Butler] made a miraculous play and things didn't work out."

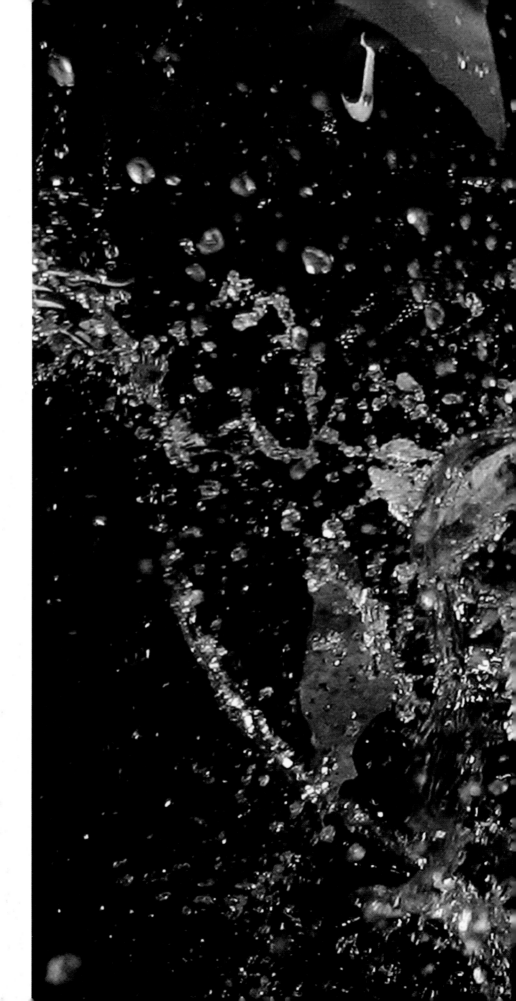

Patriots head coach
Bill Belichick receives
a dousing from his
players after New
England clinched its
fourth Super Bowl with
a 28-24 victory over
Seattle.

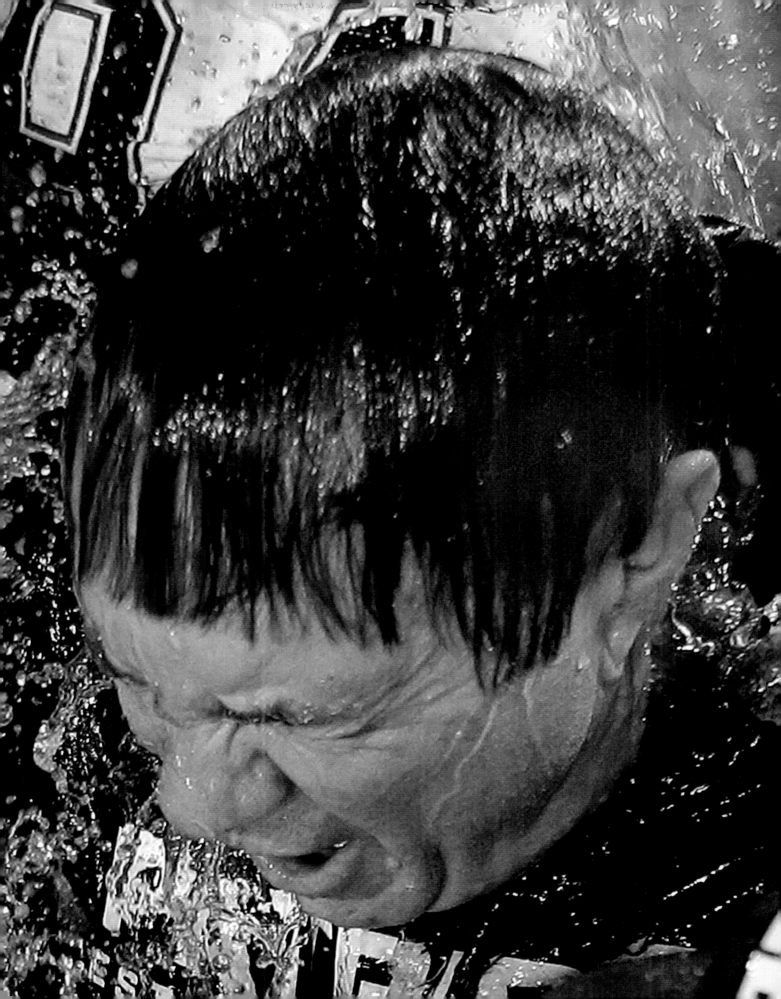

'I KNOW WE'VE HAD SOME UPS AND DOWNS THIS YEAR, BUT RIGHT NOW WE'RE UP, BABY.'

TOM BRADY · PATRIOTS QB

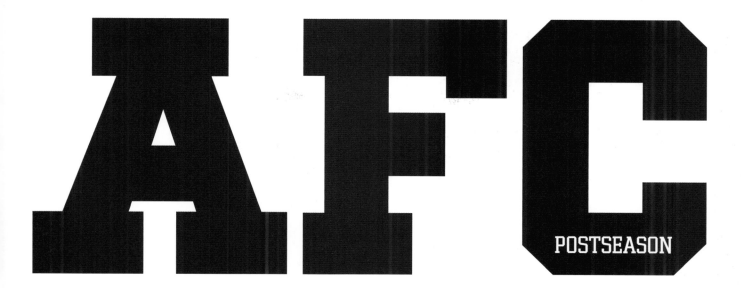

AFC

POSTSEASON

BY KEVIN PAUL DUPONT / Globe Staff

The only question remaining, even with 10 minutes left in the fourth quarter, was what would be the size of the winning margin. The Patriots already were in front, 45-7, and over on the sideline Tom Brady and Julian Edelman shared a handshake, smiles, and confident nods.

» They were going back to the Super Bowl, gifted a playoff E-ZPass by the eager-yet-not-ready-for-prime-time Indianapolis Colts. » "You don't expect this kind of result," said special teams star Matthew Slater, following yet another patented thrashing of the Colts. "It kind of catches you off guard ... but we'll take it, don't get me wrong." » Past performance indeed may not predict future results, but such was not the case at soggy Gillette on a January night fitting for Duck Boats as transit. The Colts, who could have used lifeboats, were unable to muster much offense, but their greatest fault, again, was their inability to stop the run. In the week leading up to the AFC title game, they had talked proudly about improvement in their tackling game, only to show up unable to get a grip. » Exhibit A: a total of 40 Patriot rushes that produced 177 yards and three touchdowns, most of that haul logged by powerhouse returnee LeGarrette Blount. Already the owner of a four-TD run effort against the Colts last year, he added three more, rushing a club-record 30 times for 148 yards (4.9 average). » The Colts earlier »37

6

Number of Super Bowl appearances
for the Patriots in 14 years, making them the first NFL
team to reach 6 in a 14-year period.

7

Career playoff touchdowns for LeGarrette Blount
after he scored three times against the Colts, tying him with
David Givens for most TDs in Patriots playoff history.

9

Starts in a conference championship game by Tom Brady,
most in NFL history. Brady broke a tie with Charlie Waters
(Dallas) and Jack Reynolds (LA Rams/SF).

10

Interceptions by the Patriots in the
four games they have played against Andrew Luck
of the Colts.

11

Conference championship games for
New England. The Pats improved to 8-3,
including 5-1 at home.

28

Tom Brady played in his Patriot record 28th postseason
game. Tedy Bruschi is second with 22. Vince Wilfork tied
Troy Brown and Matt Light for third-most (20).

38

Margin of victory over the Colts, the largest in
franchise history for a playoff game, topping the 45-10
victory over Denver in 2012.

51

Game-time temperature at Gillette Stadium (relative
humidity 71%), 31 degrees warmer than the 20 degrees for
the Divisional Round game vs. Baltimore.

»FROM 33 • in the playoffs had dismissed Cincinnati and Denver, but they had no answer for New England's Blount force.

"I just wanted to come and run as hard as I can," said Blount. "My offensive line is amazing. To be honest, I probably should have had more out there — I think I missed a couple of holes. We came in and planned to run the football, and whatever was working, we were going to do it."

Truth was, there was precious little that didn't work, including yet another sleight-of-hand move on the offensive line in which the Pats made behemoth tackle Nate Solder an eligible receiver for a play and then promptly turned Solder into the owner of his first and only TD pass from Brady.

Solder, left wide open on the left side, collected Brady's soft-serve toss (hold the sprinkles) into his mammoth hands, and hauled toward the goal line like a barreling 18-wheeler. After crashing over for what would be a 24-7 lead early in the third, he was met in the end zone by rejoicing fellow linemen Dan Connolly and Sebastian Vollmer.

"Amazing to be part of a game like that," said the smiling Solder, "and a cool play like that ... just amazing. I practiced that for years and ... there it is. It was just the right moment. The stars were aligned. Amazing."

"Nate's a good athlete," added defensive back Devin McCourty. "There are a lot of times he'll walk through here and you cannot tell the difference between him and Gronk walking through the locker room. The thing I loved was Nate got up like he knew he was going to score, like he'd been there before."

Be ready for anything, said Solder, when asked what he was told during the week while preparing for the Colts.

"Catch the ball," he said, when asked what he was thinking when the play was called. "Catch the ball. Hold it. Don't fumble it."

The Patriots' clever use of eligible and ineligible receivers had helped them dismiss Baltimore a week earlier and it equally flustered the Colts, who time and again heard No. 71, offensive lineman Cameron Fleming, was reporting in as the dodge artist du jour. As the night played out, the Colts' futility mounted, to the point that one half expected to hear over the PA, "The Colts, Nos. 1 through 99, report ineligible."

"We had all three phases of the »40

45-7

IND	0	7	0	0
NE	14	3	21	7

Tom Brady gets a good push from his teammates, led by James Develin, to convert a fourth-and-1 late in the first half.

»FROM 37 • game going," said Slater. "We got off to a good start. There was that big turnover there by the special teams, and that gave us a boost."

The early turnover came via the Pats' first punt, after a drive stalled out at midfield. The Colts' returner Josh Cribbs muffed the punt, the Pats taking over at the Indianapolis 26, and only six plays later Blount crashed over from the 1-yard line for the first of his TDs.

"We didn't expect it to go the way it did," said Slater, even though history once again proved precursor. "We were fortunate to get up early, put our foot on the gas, and play the game we were all looking for."

Nate Solder (77) lumbers 16 yards for his first NFL touchdown, and Jamie Collins (91) vaults over Andrew Luck after a late interception.

LeGarrette Blount touches down in the end zone for the second of his three scores, which gave the Patriots a 37-7 lead.

DEFLATE

They call it Deflategate. Get it? We're supposed to think it's like Watergate, as if a professional football team trying to cheat a little is the same as a president doing to the Constitution what Mitt Romney's poor dog did to the car roof.

If this wasn't all being taken so seriously, it would be funny. Actually, it is funny, watching grown men from the Viagra Generation go on national TV and talk about deflated balls without a hint of irony.

The stentorian tone of some of these clowns calls to mind Will Ferrell's Ron Burgundy. Except that Ferrell looks too much like Steelers quarterback Ben Roethlisberger, which sort of ruins the whole vibe. Roethlisberger was suspended for four games a few years back after a 20-year-old college student said he plied her with drinks, then raped her in the bathroom of a bar.

But, then, what's sexual assault compared with deflating footballs?

Funny, but I don't remember nearly as much a hullabaloo ensuing when it became obvious that retired NFL players are killing themselves because of the repeated concussions that are endemic to a game in which players, armored up like Army Humvees, act as guided missiles.

True, there seemed to be some incandescent rage, especially from people who wouldn't know a post pattern from a post office, after Baltimore Ravens running back Ray Rice punched out his then fiancee in an elevator last year. But then the NFL pulled a Rosemary Woods (Watergate!) by not erasing, but instead not finding the tape. They put out some public service announcements about how it's not cool to hit women and moved on. And so did most fans, to the next game.

Given the usual stuff that passes for scandal in the NFL — sexual assault, domestic violence, illegal gun possession, assorted felonies — the luxury of being able to obsess about how many pounds per square inch are pumped into or out of a football smells like ... victory.

For the NFL, this is Deflectgate, an opportunity to pretend it cares more about the integrity of the game than its $45 billion net worth.

As for our beloved hometown Patriots, they get what they deserve. Their record of being the best franchise in the NFL this millennium speaks for itself. You don't get to six Super Bowls in 14 years without being a great organization.

But the national obsession with hating the Patriots goes well beyond wins and losses. When you strip away all the bells and whistles and self-aggrandizing critics, the hyenas are baying because the Patriots, especially their head coach, are seen by much of the country as arrogant.

For all the jealousy and envy directed at Tom Brady — he's got a beautiful, rich wife, too — it pales compared with the venom aimed at Patriots coach Bill Belichick, whose cheerless, painful postgame press conferences should be titled, "I Can't Wait to Get Away From All You Morons."

Belichick got caught cheating in 2007, when the Patriots were stealing defensive signals from the New York Jets. What's striking both about Spygate then and Deflategate now is that the supposed advantage gained seems negligible compared with the potential downside. They seem more like acts of arrogance than malevolence. But then, arrogant people do stupid stuff all the time, thinking they won't get caught or, worse, not really caring what people would think if they do get caught.

Still, listening to the over-the-top rhetoric from every corner of the continent and beyond has actually engendered my sympathy. Not if, in fact, the Patriots cheated. But because of the shameless self-importance and preening self-righteousness of the Patriots' most vocal critics.

Deflategate is a grossly exaggerated morality play, an Oliver Stone script, a media event created by many who want you to believe that football is a metaphor for life, a mirror to our collective national soul.

But football's just a game, a diversion from a far messier real world, a game in which incredibly talented and conditioned athletes are merely modern and much better compensated gladiators.

And, like the Romans, we run to the coliseum.

KEVIN CULLEN • *Globe Staff*

GATE

ROOTED IN SPYGATE

Deflategate, the moniker given to the NFL's investigation into whether the Patriots used under-inflated footballs, is a source of fascination, debate, and, in some corners, indignation because it's the Patriots. A team that has enjoyed uncommon success since 2001 operates under the suspicion that it is using uncommon and untoward means to do so. That's the Patriots' own fault and the NFL's.

This latest rules controversy is the residue of Spygate. That controversy's fingerprints are all over this one, which is pumped up, even if the Patriots are guilty. (The incident was still under investigation as this book went to press.)

You remember Spygate, the embarrassing revelation that the Patriots had been taping opposing teams' signals from the sideline. The Patriots got busted during the 2007 season opener in the Meadowlands against the Jets; the NFL fined coach Bill Belichick $500,000, the team $250,000, and docked the club its 2008 first-round pick.

Being labeled a cheater is the self-inflicted wound the Patriots and Belichick, who has won more playoff games than any coach in NFL history, have to bear. Belichick will pursue any competitive advantage. Gray isn't just the color of his hoodie. It's the area he operates in.

He is an inveterate planner and a bit of a Nixonian control freak, so he pushes the boundaries. Outside of New England his stolid manner and deadpan news conferences make him an object of contempt. Any chance to nail his headset to the wall is greeted with glee, nationally.

As Wilt Chamberlain once famously said, "Nobody roots for Goliath." That's especially true if people feel Goliath is playing by his own rules.

The NFL did the Patriots no favors in Spygate by destroying the evidence it collected in 2007, evidence that could have corroborated what Belichick told Patriots owner Robert Kraft: that on a scale of 1 to 100 the impact the taping had on winning was 1. In the absence of evidence, people will believe what they want to believe about Spygate, including that it's the only reason the Patriots won any Super Bowls (absurd) and that it's part of a wider scheme of nefarious tactics used in New England. There is, thanks to NFL commissioner Roger Goodell, no concrete proof to dispel the most far-fetched conspiracies.

That brings us back to Deflategate, which is kind of fitting considering that the Patriots-Colts AFC title game was about as close as the Richard Nixon-George McGovern presidential election of 1972.

It's hard to fathom that anyone in the Colts organization truly believes they lost by 38 points because of improperly inflated footballs.

They lost because their young franchise quarterback, Andrew Luck, was completely overwhelmed, and their defense was completely overrun, again. Like the Patriots' footballs, Indianapolis got smaller on the big stage.

Governor Charlie Baker was asked about the controversy and delivered an answer coated in double entendre that left reporters laughing.

"There is just no good place to go when you're talking about allegedly deflated balls," Baker said. Baker took the issue about as seriously as it deserves to be taken. But for the Patriots, allegations of bending the rulebook to fit their needs never will be a laughing matter. Spygate and Goodell made sure of that.

CHRISTOPHER L. GASPER • *Globe Staff*

FLAG
ON THE PLAY?

'I WOULD NOT SAY THAT I'M THE MONA LISA VITO OF THE FOOTBALL WORLD.'
BILL BELICHICK

'I'M NOT SQUEEZING THE BALLS. THAT'S NOT PART OF MY PROCESS.'
TOM BRADY

'WHEN THE NFL INVESTIGATES, THEY ALWAYS GET IT RIGHT.'
JIMMY KIMMEL • TALK-SHOW HOST

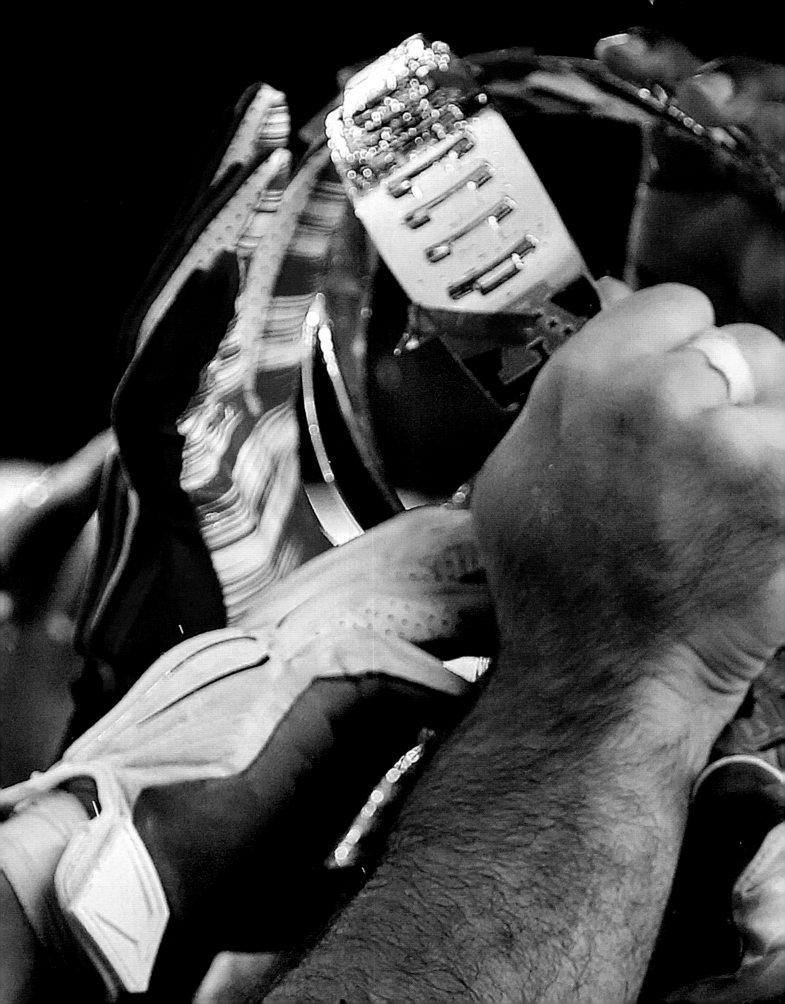

Many hands made light work of the Colts, and the Patriots hoisted their eighth AFC Championship Trophy.

'YOU'VE GOT TO GIVE CREDIT TO THEM. THEY DON'T PANIC, THEY JUST PLAY THE GAME AND KEEP AT IT, KEEP AT IT.'

JOE FLACCO · RAVENS QB

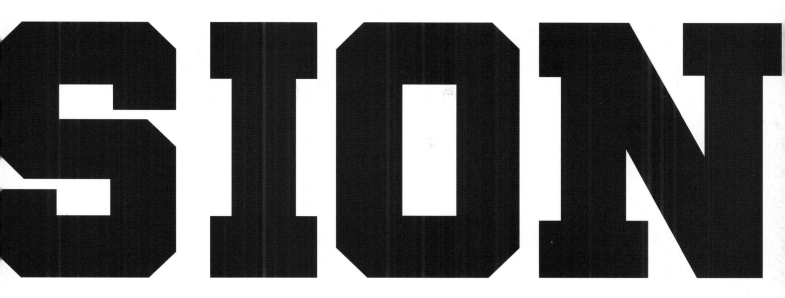

SION

BY CHRISTOPHER L. GASPER / Globe Staff

There will come a time when Tom Brady is old and gray and faded like an old photograph. In those days, we will look back upon games like the Jan. 10 playoff contest with the Baltimore Ravens wistfully, appreciating just what a luxury it was to have No. 12 at quarterback. » The Patriots don't squeak by and advance in a 35-31 instant classic of an AFC divisional playoff game at Gillette Stadium without Brady, who twice rallied the Patriots from a 14-point deficit to author the largest playoff comeback in franchise history. » All that talk all season about the improved Patriots defense giving Brady the leeway to not enter a playoff game with the mind-set that he had to score 30 points to win was proven correct. Brady didn't need 30 points to punch the Patriots' ticket to a fourth straight AFC title game. He needed 35 and dry ice in his veins on the winning fourth-quarter drive. Brady might be in decline, but if it weren't for him, the Patriots would be reclining in their La-Z-Boys right now. » Brady threw a 23-yard touchdown pass to Brandon LaFell with 5:13 to go to put the Ravens in the Patriots' rearview mirror for good. It was the 46th playoff touchdown pass of his career, moving him past his boyhood idol, Joe Montana, for the most in NFL history. » But Brady's NFL-record 19th playoff win didn't come easily. » Baltimore, which led, 31-28, with 10:17 to go, pushed »52

2

Touchdown catches for Danny Amendola, the first two-TD game of his six-year career. He had one TD catch in the 2014 regular season.

5

Career postseason rushing touchdowns by Tom Brady, who ran one in vs. the Ravens. That ties him with Curtis Martin for second-most rushing TDs by a Patriot.

8

Wins in the Divisional Round by the Patriots after a bye week in the Belichick era, against one loss.

14

Points the Patriots trailed by, twice (14-0, 28-14). They became the first team in NFL postseason history to overcome two 14-point deficits.

14

Rushing yards for New England, on 13 carries, the fewest rushing yards for a winning team in NFL postseason history.

46

Tom Brady's touchdown pass to Brandon LaFell was his third of the game and gave him a record 46 career playoff TD throws, one more than Joe Montana.

51

Yardage of scoring pass from Julian Edelman to Danny Amendola, the longest touchdown pass by a non-QB in NFL postseason history.

100

Number of all-time victories for the Patriots at Gillette Stadium after their win over Baltimore, against 19 losses.

FROM 49 • Brady and the Patriots to the precipice of playoff disaster. Brady stared down at the abyss and, with some help from creative play-calling by Bill Belichick and offensive coordinator Josh McDaniels, pulled the Patriots back.

"I can't say enough about Tom Brady," said guard Ryan Wendell, who had to slide over to center when Bryan Stork got injured in the first half. "There is a reason why everybody knows his name. The guy knows what he is doing, and Tom is competitive. He doesn't let anything get him down. He always comes back and does his job."

Coming into this game, all of the talk was about Joe Flacco's playoff oeuvre. Flacco came in having won an NFL-record seven road playoff games. He hadn't thrown a playoff interception in 166 attempts and had 13 touchdowns and no picks in his previous five playoff games.

Flacco (292 yards with four TDs and two interceptions) was good. But Brady, who was 33 of 50 for a franchise-playoff-record 367 yards, with three TDs and one interception, was the quarterback worthy of a playoff pedestal when it mattered most.

On the go-ahead drive, Brady was 8 of 9 for 72 yards. The lone ball to hit the turf was by design, a throwaway.

"It felt like a long day in practice. Everybody is tired and everybody is complaining, and you look at Tom and he's just calm," said LaFell of the final drive. "He is putting us in the right places. He is just going out there spreading the ball around and making plays for us."

Brady was required to make a lot of plays in the second half; he didn't hand off once, in what may have been the most lopsided offensive game plan in team history. The Patriots threw the ball on 26 of their first 27 plays of the second half against the league's No. 4-ranked run defense.

Brady hadn't enjoyed much success against the rakish Ravens in the playoffs. He came in 1-2 against Baltimore, completing 56 percent of his passes and throwing three touchdowns and seven interceptions.

Early on, it looked like it would be more of the same as the Patriots »55

35–31

BAL	14	7	7	3
NE	7	7	14	7

Tom Brady tumbles into the end zone after a 4-yard scramble to cut the Patriots' deficit to 14-7.

Julian Edelman (11), a quarterback in college, uncorks his first NFL pass, a 51-yard strike to Danny Amendola (80) that brought the Patriots even at 28–28. "He throws it better than I do," said Tom Brady later.

FROM 52 • fell into a 14-0 hole against Playoff Joe and the unflappable Ravens. The Patriots were outgained, 145-16, in that span.

Brady showed early on he was willing to sacrifice his body. On third and goal from the Ravens' 4, Brady took it himself, beating Baltimore linebacker Daryl Smith to the end zone.

Hearts started beating again across New England. They were fluttering with excitement after Brady threw a tying TD pass to Danny Amendola with 3:37 left in the half.

The naysayers who claim that Brady has lost the clutch touch got some ammunition right before the half. Brady locked on to Rob Gronkowski with hungry eyes and threw an inexcusable interception at the Baltimore 43 with 63 seconds left in the half. That led to a Flacco TD pass to Owen Daniels with 10 seconds left to go up, 21-14.

Brady was captured by the NBC cameras on the sideline with his head in his hands in distress.

"Yeah, it was a terrible play by me," said Brady. "I just made a terrible decision."

Another Super Bowl-title-less season appeared to be on the horizon after Flacco hit an uncovered Justin Forsett to put Baltimore up, 28-14, with 10:22 left in the third.

Then the Patriots dug into their bag of tricks, confounding the Ravens and the officials.

Brady hit Gronkowski for a 5-yard score with 6:48 to go in the third, and just 2:28 later the Patriots tied the game on another touchdown pass. But this one wasn't thrown by Brady. Brady threw a lateral to wide receiver Julian Edelman, a quarterback at Kent State, and Edelman hit a wide-open Amendola for a 51-yard score and a tie.

"He throws it better than I do," said Brady. "He spun it. It was a perfect spiral, right in stride. We have to make some rules that he can't throw it better than I can. He did."

That bit of passing prestidigitation was a prelude to a heart-stopping fourth quarter, when Brady delivered once again.

SOLDER

HOOMANAWANUI

SIYGATE

OK, let's try to explain that crazy receiver-ineligible formation from the Patriots' win over the Ravens, and how Bill Belichick just may have unlocked the door to a wild new offense with infinite possibilities.

We'll start with the basics:

On each play, an offense is required to have seven players line up directly on the line of scrimmage, and four behind it. The quarterback is one of those four, and the others are usually running backs, fullbacks, tight ends, and slot receivers.

Six of the 11 players on offense are eligible receivers and can catch a forward pass. The other five are ineligible receivers. They cannot catch a forward pass or head downfield before the ball. But they can receive and advance a lateral. This is important.

Of the seven players on the line of scrimmage, only the two on either end are eligible receivers. The inside players are all ineligible. This is also important.

Players at positions that are typically eligible (quarterback, running back, fullback, receiver,

tight end) wear Nos. 1-49 and 80-89. Players at positions that are typically ineligible (offensive line) wear Nos. 50-79. Players are free to report as eligible, and vice versa. They just need to report to the referee before each play. A player is free to report as eligible/ineligible on consecutive plays, but he needs to inform the referee each time. Once a player changes his eligibility, he only returns to his original eligibility if he sits out a play or after a timeout, end of a quarter, after a penalty, and so on.

The Patriots used this tactic three times in the third quarter in the middle of a drive. They pulled right guard Josh Kline from the game, lined up Nate Solder at left guard, Michael Hoomanawanui at left tackle, and inserted a skill player as ineligible.

The first time, Shane Vereen was ineligible. He was lined up in the right slot, but on the line of scrimmage. Standing to his right was Julian Edelman, also on the line of scrimmage. Vereen was considered an "inside" player and therefore not eligible.

On the left side of the formation were Danny Amendola and Brandon LaFell, both lined up off the line of scrimmage. That made Hoomanawanui the "outside" player on the left, making him eligible, even though he lined up at tackle.

The Ravens had no idea what was going on, and Tom Brady found Hoomanawanui for 16 yards. Two plays later Brady hit Edelman for 11 yards, and two plays after that went back to Hoomanawanui for 14 yards before John Harbaugh finally threw a fit and drew an unsportsmanlike conduct penalty.

The first two times the Patriots used the tactic, Vereen and Hoomanawanui came off the field on the following play. The third time, a penalty allowed Vereen to stay on the field for the next play.

Future Patriots opponents will be wary of this formation. But it was a brilliant tactic, and proved once again why Belichick is the greatest coach of his generation.

SHALISE MANZA YOUNG
Globe Staff

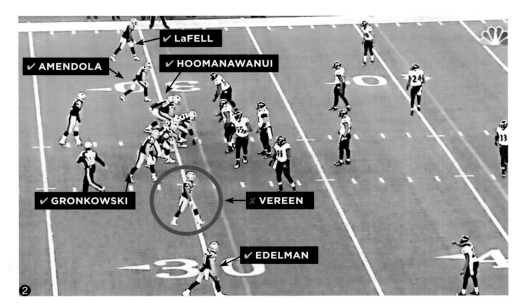

- ✔ LaFELL
- ✔ AMENDOLA
- ✔ HOOMANAWANUI
- ✔ GRONKOWSKI
- ✗ VEREEN
- ✔ EDELMAN

❷

- VEREEN

❸

- HOOMANAWANUI

❹

FLAG
ON THE PLAY?

❶ Right guard Josh Kline left the field. Nate Solder is now the left guard and Michael Hoomanawanui the left tackle.

❷ The Patriots have six offensive skill players in the game (excluding QB Tom Brady), but only five can be eligible receivers. By rule, the three players off the line of scrimmage — Brandon LaFell, Danny Amendola, and Rob Gronkowski — are eligible receivers, and Julian Edelman and Hoomanawanui are both eligible because they are the outside players standing on the line of scrimmage. Shane Vereen is ineligible because he's on the inside of the line of scrimmage.

❸ Hoomanawanui is eligible to streak down the field for the pass, even though he lined up at the left tackle position. Vereen, meanwhile, cannot go downfield, or else he'll be penalized as an ineligible receiver.

❹ The Ravens have no idea what hit them, and Hoomanawanui gets a nice 16-yard gain.

'IT'S A SUBSTITUTION TYPE OF A TRICK TYPE OF A THING.'

JOHN HARBAUGH · RAVENS COACH

'MAYBE THESE GUYS GOTTA STUDY THE RULE BOOK AND FIGURE IT OUT.'

TOM BRADY

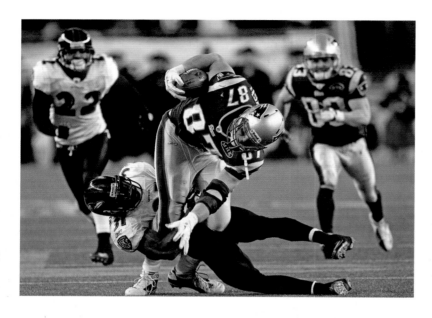

Rob Gronkowski (87) caught seven passes for 108 yards and a score. Safety Patrick Chung broke up an end-zone throw to Baltimore tight end Owen Daniels (81). Brandon LaFell (19) hauled in the game-winning reception with 5:21 to play.

Patriots' defensive back Duron Harmon (30) thwarts Ravens' wide receiver Torrey Smith by coming up with a late interception to help seal the New England win.

A plethora of Patriots batted away the last-gasp throw of Ravens' quarterback Joe Flacco to preserve New England's narrow victory.

'THEY'RE NOT GOOD ANYMORE. THEY'RE WEAK.'

TRENT DILFER · ESPN ANALYST, TWEETING AFTER PATRIOTS' WEEK 4 LOSS

'WE'RE ON TO CINCINNATI.'

BILL BELICHICK · PATRIOTS COACH

SON

BY BEN VOLIN / GLOBE STAFF

The Patriots ended the 2014 NFL season at the pinnacle of their sport, hoisting the Lombardi Trophy for the fourth time and cementing Bill Belichick and Tom Brady as the greatest coach-quarterback duo of all time. » But this championship season was not your typical wire-to-wire domination. Before finishing on top, there was shock, frustration, and controversy to overcome. » The first shock came right before the season, when popular captain and locker room leader Logan Mankins was dealt to Tampa Bay. » Then, in Week 4, they were pasted by the Kansas City Chiefs, 41-14, on "Monday Night Football." Brady watched the final eight minutes of the game from the bench, his head hung low. Patriots haters from coast to coast reveled in the team's misery and 2-2 record. » "It might be the worst beating that I've had as an owner," Robert Kraft would later say. "Definitely in the [15-year] Belichick era." » But, believe it or not, that was the night that Belichick knew he had a championship team. The Patriots kept fighting hard despite the lopsided score and the tough road conditions. » "I think that was a good sign. Not that we played well, but we played hard," Belichick said. "I think at that point we all kind of realized that if we could just play well and just combine that with our physical and mental toughness, that we could be OK." » The Patriots moved #OnToCincinnati. »99

5

The Patriots earned the No. 1 playoff seed in the AFC for the fifth time (2003, 2007, 2010, 2011, and 2014).

8.0

Number of sacks by Rob Ninkovich, which led the team. Chandler Jones and Donta Hightower were next with 6.0 each.

9.6

The Patriots' point differential for the season, best in the NFL. They averaged 29.2 points a game and allowed 19.6.

12

Second-half points allowed by the Patriots in their final six games. They did not allow a second-half TD after Nov. 16 at Indianapolis.

+12

The Patriots' turnover differential, which trailed only Green Bay (+14) and tied Houston for the best in the AFC.

35

Consecutive home wins vs. the AFC, an NFL record for conference wins, ended Dec. 28 by Buffalo. The Pats had previously lost at home to an AFC team in 2008.

94.6

Stephen Gostkowski's field-goal percentage (35 of 37), giving him a total of 156 points, which led the league.

412

Team-leading rushing yards by Jonas Gray, the second-fewest to ever lead the team in a season (Jim Nance's 321 yards in 1965 is the lowest).

DOLPHINS

9/7/14 ● MIAMI

It was as if the Miami Dolphins took one of those CSI black lights to the Patriots and what had looked like a tidy, clean, pristine Super Bowl contender suddenly looked like a spotty outfit that needed to be cleaned up pronto, like Tom Brady's grass-stain-filled uniform.

After an offseason full of anticipation and a preseason loaded with lofty predictions, the Patriots fell flat when the curtain went up at Sun Life Stadium, getting shut out in the second half to lose, 33-20, to the Dolphins.

It was the first time the Patriots lost a season opener since they were annihilated, 31-0, by the Buffalo Bills in 2003, following the exiling of safety Lawyer Milloy.

The cause of the Patriots' Opening Day demise was an inability to control the play in the trenches. Paging Logan Mankins.

The NFL isn't fantasy football, where you win with skill-position players. The line of scrimmage is ground zero for victory and the aftershocks from the Patriots' inability to hold their ground on either side of the ball there reverberated throughout the whole team.

South Beach nightclubs have lines that are tougher to get through than the ones the Patriots presented in Game 1.

The Dolphins neutered the New England offense in the second half — holding it to just 67 yards on 37 plays — by overrunning the Patriots' patchwork, Mankins-free offensive line.

Miami sacked Brady four times, two of them Cameron Wake strip-sacks. TB12 was constantly out of time and under siege. Maybe I'm wrong, but isn't keeping Brady upright in the best interests of the team?

Meanwhile, the Dolphins' offensive line, which had five new starters, pushed the Patriots around, clearing the way for Miami to rush for 191 yards and average 5 yards a rush.

Miami outgained the Patriots, 222-67, in the second half.

There was so much focus on the Patriots' upgraded pass defense with Darrelle Revis that nobody worried about the run.

"Any time somebody can run the ball like that it's not good," said Patriots defensive lineman Vince Wilfork. "We have to go back to the drawing board."

"I think our execution was just terrible," said Brady, who was held to 10 of 27 for 62 yards passing in the second half. "We just couldn't do anything offensively. We couldn't sustain drives, and we couldn't get a first down. We couldn't run it. We couldn't throw it. It was just a bad day."

»CHRISTOPHER L. GASPER

33-20

NE	10	10	0	0
MIA	7	3	13	10

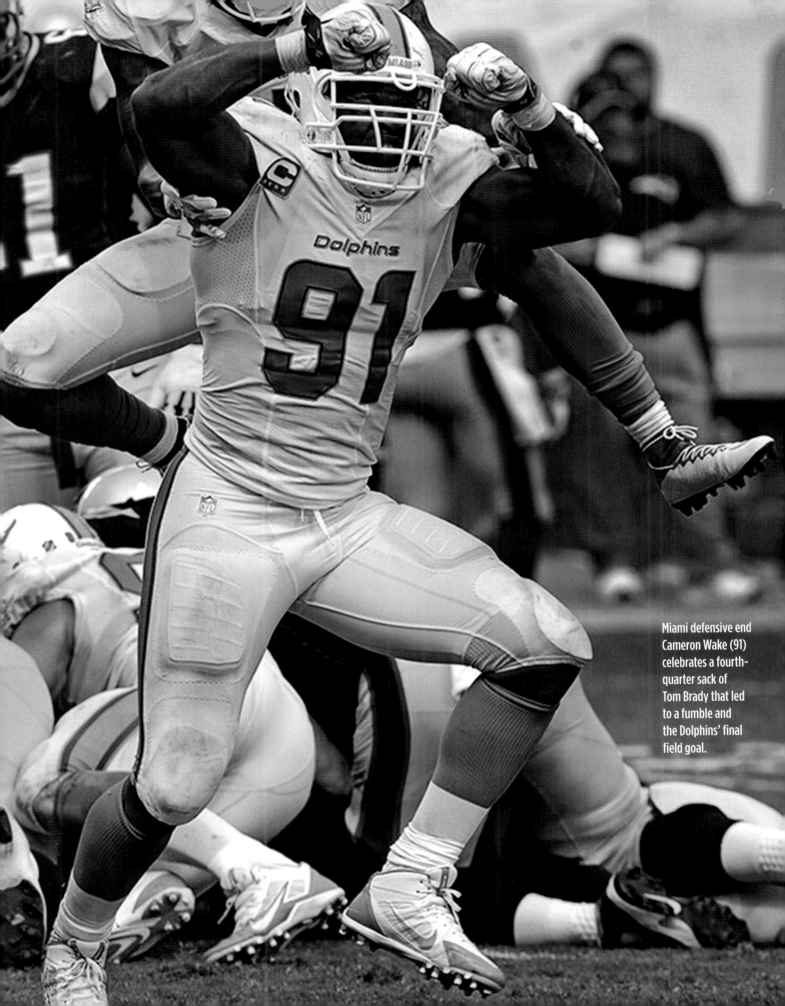

Miami defensive end Cameron Wake (91) celebrates a fourth-quarter sack of Tom Brady that led to a fumble and the Dolphins' final field goal.

9/14/14 ● MINNEAPOLIS
During this game against the Patriots, things got so bad for Matt Cassel, the Vikings quarterback of the present, that fans at TCF Bank Stadium began calling for Teddy Bridgewater, the team's quarterback of the future.

Cassel, essentially holding the seat warm until Bridgewater, a first-round pick this year, is ready to take over, had an utterly forgettable performance against his former team, throwing four interceptions, three of which led to points for the Patriots.

Throw in some improved special teams play, including a blocked field goal returned for a touchdown, and the Patriots looked much better during their 30-7 victory against the Vikings than they did a week earlier in a lackluster effort against the Dolphins.

The Patriots avoided their first 0-2 start since the 2001 season, and the victory was the 200th in the regular season for Bill Belichick as a head coach, making him just the sixth to reach that milestone.

Week 2 was about rebounding: About the Patriots rebounding from their loss to Miami; about the special teams unit atoning for its poor outing against the Dolphins; and even about the defense rebounding from a terrible opening series in which the Vikings marched 80 yards in seven plays to take a 7-0 lead.

Team captain Devin McCourty said he knew the Patriots would bounce back the day after their season-opening loss, when they began preparing for the Vikings.

Fellow captain Vince Wilfork agreed.

"I thought we had a great week of practice, we prepared well, and it showed today," Wilfork said. "Guys came to work. We didn't have our heads held low coming off an awful loss."

The Vikings were without star running back Adrian Peterson, who was deactivated because he was arrested and charged with reckless or negligent injury of a child.

Wilfork was actually disappointed the Patriots didn't get to face Peterson.

"He's one of the best in the game at that position," Wilfork said. "Coming off a performance like we did at Miami [allowing 193 rushing yards on 35 carries to Knowshon Moreno and Lamar Miller combined], we thought it was a big deal for us to face another guy, one of the best in the league, to see where we're at defensively. But the way we played today, I think we played very well."

A relaxed Belichick said, "That was a real great team win for us today. We got contributions from all three areas. Offensively we had a more balanced attack than we had last week, which is what we needed. Defensively we had a lot of turnovers, plus the blocked kick. That's a good formula."

»SHALISE MANZA YOUNG

30-7

NE	10	14	3	3
MIN	7	0	0	0

Logan Ryan (26) evades a tackle after his third-quarter interception, one of four picks by the Patriots of former New England QB Matt Cassel.

9/21/14 ● FOXBOROUGH

The Patriots' home opener against the Oakland Raiders should have been sponsored by Ambien.

That New England's 16-9 victory came down to a holding penalty on the Raiders that negated the tying touchdown, immediately followed by a pinball interception that landed in the large mitts of Vince Wilfork with less than a minute remaining, was a testament to both the Patriots' current offensive futility and the Raiders' institutionalized ineptitude.

Not even Tom Brady, whose measurements are already known by the folks at the Pro Football Hall of Fame, can make this offense dynamic. It is as prosaic as the Patriots have had in years.

When coach Bill Belichick says the Patriots have to block it better, throw it better, run it better, coach it better, and hydrate before the game better, he's not stonewalling. He's being honest.

This offense struggled to produce the Patriots' customary style points and points in general.

The wide receivers not named Julian Edelman couldn't consistently get open and posed no deep threat. The offensive line couldn't give Brady time. In Week 3, it also couldn't create running room against a Raiders defense that came in ranked dead last in the league in run defense (New England rushed 32 times for 76 yards).

It's not a good sign when one of the best blocks was delivered by Brady, who cut down Carlos Rogers in the fourth quarter after Shane Vereen reversed field to pick up 5 yards.

It's clear that the 37-year-old Brady can't avoid the rush as well as he used to. There is … wait for it … decline in that area. But pinning all the blame for a scuffling offense on the franchise quarterback is like labeling your Bentley a lemon for failing to start when you didn't put any gas in it.

Raiders defensive lineman Antonio Smith said you can't blame Brady for all of the offense's ills.

"If they could protect him, Brady is Brady," said Smith. "I don't think Brady has lost nothing. Brady is Brady, and the way he runs the game is still effective."

Brady finished a respectable 24 of 37 for 234 yards, with a second-quarter touchdown toss to Rob Gronkowski. But he was sacked twice and hit six times, including getting plastered by old friend Justin Tuck in the fourth quarter after left tackle Nate Solder whiffed like Jackie Bradley Jr.

After the game Brady told Tuck he got him good. That summed up the day.

»CHRISTOPHER L. GASPER

16-9

OAK	3	0	6	0
NE	0	10	0	6

Vince Wilfork, whose interception on a deflected pass clinched the Patriots' win, joins Raiders' offensive tackle Melenik Watson post-game.

9/29/14 ● KANSAS CITY, MO
Forget being "all in" this season. In Week 4, the Patriots were all out — all out of answers for a leaky offensive line, all out of excuses for suiting up Danny Amendola, and all out of "In Belichick We Trust" platitudes to explain gaping roster holes.

The team that's not "all in" couldn't get out of Arrowhead Stadium fast enough after getting its doors blown off in a game they were never in.

The Patriots were trampled and humiliated, 41-14, by the Kansas City Chiefs in a Monday night game, dropping to an unimpressive 2-2 on the season. New England's two victories are over the Minnesota Vikings, who were shellshocked in the wake of Adrian Peterson's child abuse imbroglio, and the Oakland Raiders, the NFL's perpetual black hole.

This was the second-largest margin of defeat for the Patriots during the Bill Belichick era, topped only by the infamous Lawyer Milloy Game, a season-opening 31-0 loss to the Buffalo Bills in 2003.

"They all count the same in the standings. There is no way you feel good after a game like that,

whenever it is," said Belichick of the prime-time pummeling his team endured.

The Patriots trailed, 17-0, at the half, 24-0 after Tom Brady was strip-sacked in the third quarter by Tamba Hali to set up Jamaal Charles's third touchdown of the game, and 27-0 after Brady was intercepted by Sean Smith on the ensuing possession.

It was 41-7 after Chiefs safety Husain Abdullah returned a Brady interception 39 yards for a touchdown with 10:34 left. That was the last pass TB12 (14 of 23 for 159 yards with one touchdown, two interceptions, and two fumbles) threw. He was pulled for Jimmy Garoppolo.

"When you lose the way we lost there is not a lot be gained other than the feeling that we have now and that we don't want this feeling again," said Brady. "We've had it before. It's motivated us ... This is a tough one."

Arrowhead was full of sound and fury signifying the Patriots' futility.

"I think the biggest thing we're going to take away from this game is we've got to play a lot better if we're going to be a good team and win games," said Patriots safety Devin McCourty. "I'm disappointed, as this is the most embarrassing game I've ever been a part of. We lost in every aspect."
»CHRISTOPHER L. GASPER

41-14

NE	0	0	7	7
KC	7	10	10	14

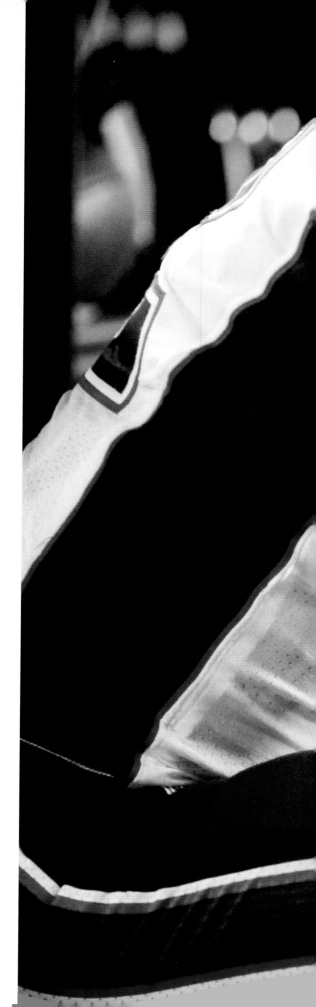

Bruised and battered (two sacks, two fumbles), Tom Brady's night was over after the Chiefs returned their second interception for a score and a 41-7 lead.

10/5/14 ● FOXBOROUGH

It's the same as it ever was for the Patriots, great quarterback play, great coaching, and another prime-time embarrassment of a pretender to the throne.

Tom Brady turned a chorus of questions about his play into a chorus of chants of his name in adulation, and the Patriots responded to a week of critiques and criticism with a vintage performance. There was no doubting Thomas or the Patriots after they drummed the Cincinnati Bengals, 43-17, at Gillette.

Crisis averted.

Don't believe for a second that the Patriots didn't hear the doubting and derision tossed their way following an embarrassing 27-point loss to the Kansas City Chiefs in Week 4. One member of the organization gleefully asked a reporter if all his stories needed to be rewritten. Ignore the noise is just a slogan.

For those waiting to revel in both Brady's and the Patriots' demise, salivating over the unraveling of the NFL's most successful quarterback-coach relationship — Brady and coach Bill Belichick — it was yet another reminder that the Patriots are a different species than the rest of the NFL.

Just when it seemed Brady and the Patriots were falling apart they put it all together in a prime-time showdown with the fraudulent Bengals, who began the game as the NFL's last undefeated team. The Patriots trounced Cincinnati by 26 points and rolled up 505 yards of offense.

On the day when his quarterback contemporary, Peyton Manning passed for a career-high 479 yards and threw four touchdowns, including the 500th of his career, Brady displayed vintage form. He was 23 of 35 for 292 yards and two touchdowns. He guided the Patriots to points on eight of 12 drives, a maestro worthy of Symphony Hall.

The first play from scrimmage was a play-action pass and Brady hit Brandon LaFell for a gain of 20. His next pass was a 30-yard gain to tight end Tim Wright. On fourth and 1 from the Bengals' 5 yard line, Brady converted a quarterback sneak to keep the drive alive. Two plays later, Stevan Ridley plowed in from a yard out to put the Patriots on top.

Cincinnati, which in its first three games of the season had trailed for a total of 48 seconds, never led in the game.

The doubted and derided franchise QB guided his team to the end zone again on the team's second drive, drilling a 17-yard touchdown pass to a streaking Wright. After his TD toss, Brady scooped up the ball, took it to the sideline, and spiked it emphatically.

"We always talk about what Patriot football is and I think you saw it tonight," said Brady.

All is right with the world again.

»CHRISTOPHER L. GASPER

43-17

CIN	0	3	14	0
NE	14	6	14	9

Kyle Arrington tumbles into the end zone to score on a fumbled Cincinnati kickoff return, giving the Patriots a 34-10 lead.

10/12/14 ● ORCHARD PARK, NY
The Buffalo Bills have energetic new owners, a refurbished Ralph Wilson Stadium, and a new long-term lease on life in western New York. But in Week 6 the rebranded Bills still lacked a key ingredient: a quarterback.

The franchise makeover wasn't enough to cover up the difference between the Bills and the Patriots, overlords of the AFC East. The real owners of the Bills, your New England Patriots, claimed sole possession of first place in the division and spoiled the era of gridiron good feelings that had enveloped Buffalo with a 37-22 dispatching of their favorite foils at The Ralph.

Bill Belichick and Tom Brady put the football down for Buffalo to kick and then pulled it away. Until Buffalo, which started retread Kyle Orton, or any of the other teams in the AFC East can close the Quarterback Gap, the division will remain property of the Patriots.

"Brady is a good guy. He is a great player, future Hall of Famer," said Bills defensive tackle Marcell Dareus. "I don't ever see them not being the Patriots that they are with him on the team. He is a good veteran. He knows how to mix things up. They'll always be the Patriots as long as he is there."

Brady and the Patriots' offense built on their 43-point offensive rebirth against Cincinnati, scoring on four second-half possessions (excluding the game-ending genuflection) to post 24 points after the break.

Brady provided another rebuttal to the endless parade of talk-show Dan Duquettes pronouncing that he was in the twilight of his career. Tom Terrific was 15 of 17 for 274 yards and three touchdowns in the second half, including a soul-crushing 56-yarder to Brandon LaFell with 2:49 to go.

Try convincing the good people of Buffalo that Brady, who finished 27 of 37 for 361 yards and four touchdowns, has fallen from the elite quarterback pedestal and can't get up.

The Patriots offensive line has taken almost as many metaphorical shots as the physical ones Brady has taken. But against Buffalo, the much-maligned men up front held down the fort after losing starting left guard Dan Connolly to a head injury in the first half.

Brady completed passes to 10 receivers. He even dusted off the deep ball, hitting training camp sensation Brian Tyms for a 43-yard touchdown on the first possession of the second half.

"That's what good offenses are," said Brady. "Whoever is out there has to produce, and guys are playing big roles. We are trying to find things that work."

The Bills bit the dust, per usual, but took a bite out of the Patriots roster, as both Jerod Mayo and Stevan Ridley suffered season-ending right knee injuries.

»CHRISTOPHER L. GASPER

37-22

NE	0	13	10	14
BUF	0	7	7	8

Tim Wright snags a
1-yard TD pass, his only
catch of the game, to
put the Patriots up, 7-0.
It was one of four TD
passes for Tom Brady.

10/16/14 ● FOXBOROUGH

It was a defeat so crushing that it almost left Rex Ryan, of all people, at a loss for words.

The words tumbled out of Ryan's mouth in his press conference after the Patriots escaped with a 27-25 victory over a New York Jets team that had outplayed them for much of the Thursday-night game. But it was clear Ryan was in no mood to talk and at a loss to explain another loss to archenemies Bill Belichick and Tom Brady.

Thanks to Patriots defensive tackle Chris Jones blocking Nick Folk's 58-yard field goal attempt with five seconds left, Ryan's Jets suffered their sixth consecutive loss and sank to 1-6 on the season.

On talent alone, Ryan's Jets had no business being in this game. But Ryan pulled the strings most of the night that allowed his shell of a team to out-execute the Patriots. It would have been easy for the Jets to be roadkill for the Patriots, but Gang Green hung around like an unwelcome house guest.

Vociferous Rex had his team ready to play on a short week. The Jets outgained the Patriots, 423 yards to 323. They ran 43 times for a season-high 218 yards. They held the ball for 40 minutes and 54 seconds. They didn't punt until there was 1:44 left in the third quarter. They committed zero turnovers. And they lost because they have a patchwork secondary and shaky young quarterback (Geno Smith).

The group Ryan brought to Gillette Stadium was talent-starved compared to the teams he beat the Patriots with three out of the first five times he played them. It has little measure of talent and little margin for error.

The Patriots' first touchdown, a 49-yard pass to Shane Vereen without a Jet in the 508 area code, came on a busted coverage between Patriots castoff cornerback Phillip Adams and Antonio Allen, a safety who has spent most of the year playing corner for the defensive-back-depleted Jets.

The play Ryan will see in his sleep came with the Patriots facing third and goal from the Jets' 19 in the fourth quarter. Brady rolled to his right and threw to forgotten wide receiver Danny Amendola, who beat Allen for a touchdown that made it 27-19 with 7:55 to go.

"The great thing about Rex is that he believes in all of us. Quite frankly, we let him down today," said outside linebacker Calvin Pace.

»CHRISTOPHER L. GASPER

27-25

NYJ	6	6	7	6
NE	7	10	3	7

Nick Folk's last-second, game-winning field goal try is blocked by New England's Chris Jones as the Patriots survive a scare from the lowly Jets.

10/26/14 ● FOXBOROUGH

Rob Gronkowski is not so much a football player as he is a force of nature that leaves devastated defenses and bruised egos in its wake. We got the Full Gronkowski in Week 8. It registered a 10 on the fun scale, unless you were a Chicago Bears defender.

The term "game changer" is overused, and Gronkowski playing at this level isn't a game changer, anyway. He is a season changer for the Patriots, who have won four straight after brushing aside the Bears, 51-23, like they were Alabama playing some Directional U.

Remember all that talk (some of it in this corner) that Tom Brady didn't have enough weapons to keep up with Peyton Manning and the Denver Broncos? There are few weapons more devastating than a healthy Gronkowski, who terrorized the Chicago defense for a career-high-tying nine catches for 149 yards and a career high-tying three touchdowns.

He is a football force on par with Calvin Johnson, A.J. Green, or Dez Bryant, and like those dynamic wideouts, he isn't covered even when he is.

It's not a coincidence the revival of the Patriots offense came as Gronkowski, returning from a torn anterior cruciate ligament in his right knee, regained his sui generis form. In the first four games of the season, Gronkowski had 13 receptions for 147 yards. In the next four, he had 27 receptions for 411 yards.

It was Gronkowski who revealed after the Patriots' vindicating victory over the Cincinnati Bengals he had been determined to make Brady look like Brady again. Aided by improved offensive line play, he had that invigorating effect on the entire offense.

A lot of football by Gronk is school-yard simple. My guy is bigger and stronger than your guy. He simply beats opponents with gridiron genetic superiority.

"Being a big guy, obviously, I'm not as fast as the DBs and the safeties, and some of the linebackers are really fast, too," said Gronkowski. "I got to use my body as leverage to outflank the guy, use it like a basketball move to box out. Sometimes, it's huge to use the body to get open."

Gronkowski caught the Patriots' first score. Brady (30 of 35 for 354 yards and five touchdowns) just lofted an alley-oop to him, and Gronkowski went up over helpless and hapless Chicago safety Ryan Mundy. It was like watching Dwight Howard rebound at your rec league hoops game. It gave Brady and Gronkowski the record for most quarterback-to-tight end touchdown connections in team history at 46.

"He is a special player," said Patriots cornerback Darrelle Revis. "They come rare. I'm happy to be his teammate."

»CHRISTOPHER L. GASPER

51-23

CHI	0	7	8	8
NE	7	31	7	6

Rob Gronkowski beats Chicago's Shea McClellin for one of his three TDs as the Pats rang up the most first-half points ever allowed by the Bears (38).

**DOLPHINS
VIKINGS
RAIDERS
CHIEFS
BENGALS
BILLS
JETS
BEARS
BRONCOS**
COLTS
LIONS
PACKERS
CHARGERS
DOLPHINS
JETS
BILLS

11/2/14 ☛ FOXBOROUGH
Here's where everything changes.

Before Game 9, the Patriots were suspect. Sure, they were 6-2, resting in their comfy spot atop the suddenly competitive Warhol, but we were waiting for a victory that would make them legit. Crushing the mail-it-in Bears at Gillette did not do the trick. Ditto for a win over the ever-ordinary Bills in Orchard Park. Beating the Bengals seemed like a big deal at the time, but that was before Marvin Lewis and his players again demonstrated their limitations.

And so we gathered at the Razor on a blustery Sunday in November and wondered if this would be the day that the Patriots would make a statement.

And they did.

New England 43, Denver 21. It was Tom Brady over Peyton Manning, Julian Edelman over Wes Welker, Rob Gronkowski over T. J. Ward ... and Bill Belichick over Grady Fox ... and Harvey Leonard. On a day that the Patriots honored players from their three Super Bowl victories, Belichick's defense played to the tune of 2003.

It's hard to believe that as recently as Sept. 29 we had

Trent Dilfer declaring that the Patriots are "not good anymore," and there was some local conversation about maybe trading Brady, who appeared to be in "serious decline." We groused about New England's swiss cheesy O-line and the arrogant trading of Logan Mankins.

This was the year when the Patriots were vulnerable. Denver "loaded up" during the offseason, spending money and acquiring big-name players. The Broncos were "all in." They were a Big Orange Machine, shedding everything in their path as they thundered into Foxborough. Manning had already broken the record for career touchdown passes and was taking his brand to a new level at the age of 38.

But Belichick is Peyton's Kryptonite. Manning is 2-11 in Foxborough. He finished with 34 completions in 57 attempts for a whopping 438 yards, but it was a garbage-time stat line.

In the first quarter, when it mattered, Manning converted only one of four third-down opportunities. In Denver's first four possessions, the Broncos had two three-and-outs (aggregate negative yardage) and Manning was intercepted once. New England's beefed-up secondary dismantled Denver's vaunted "weapons" as the Patriots built a 27-7 lead. Brady completed 33 of 53 passes for 333 yards with four touchdowns and one interception.

When it was 43-21 with 8½ minutes left in the fourth, Patriots fans chanted, "Brady's better." There was no argument from the Broncos sideline. And there was no dispute in wiseguy NFL post-game roundtables.

»DAN SHAUGHNESSY

43-21

DEN	7	0	14	0
NE	3	24	10	6

Julian Edelman spikes the ball after the first of his two TDs. His second set a career franchise record for punt return TDs (4).

11/16/14 ● INDIANAPOLIS

This was a night when Tom Brady wasn't at his best, but the Patriots were still at their best.

On the championship checklist, being able to win a tough game when the franchise quarterback is off his game is, just like the Patriots in the AFC, right at the top.

This is the team the Patriots were when they were winning Super Bowls, a Swiss Army knife that could beat you by any means necessary. They didn't need their quarterback to be perfect, flawless, or transcendent to author signature road victories.

This was a complete team win by a complete team that only needed its quarterback to be rock solid, not a rock star.

Brady was, by his lofty standards, average in his dueling No. 12s matchup with Colts passing prodigy Andrew Luck. The final numbers look good — 19 of 30 for 257 yards and two touchdowns with two interceptions, including an egregious pick late in the first half that jump-started the Colts.

But Brady was a passenger, not the driving force on this night.

The Patriots' offense, which rolled up 501 yards, was most effective when Brady was handing off, not flinging the ball down the field.

Led by the latest in a long line of Bill Belichick bargain bin finds, running back Jonas Gray, the Patriots ran for 244 yards and four touchdowns on 45 carries.

"I think you've got to be able to find different ways to win," said Brady. "Depending on the matchup that you get you've got to devise a game plan that you think is going to work. Then once you get in there, see if it works, and if it is you stay with it.

"I thought tonight we showed great toughness on both sides of the football and special teams ... It was a great win, great win on the road, against a damn good football team. They all get bigger from here."

Just like that ill-fated night in Kansas City, Brady didn't finish a prime-time road game, and came off the field for Jimmy Garoppolo in the fourth quarter. But this time it was because the team around him had picked him up, not left him exposed.

This night wasn't about Brady. It was about seeing a team that doesn't always need him to play like a superstar to go to the Super Bowl.

»CHRISTOPHER L. GASPER

42-20

NE	7	7	14	14
IND	3	7	3	7

Jonas Gray chugs past Colt defenders for his fourth touchdown of the night. Gray rushed for 201 yards as the Patriots wore down Indianapolis.

DOLPHINS
VIKINGS
RAIDERS
CHIEFS
BENGALS
BILLS
JETS
BEARS
BRONCOS
COLTS
LIONS
PACKERS
CHARGERS
DOLPHINS
JETS
BILLS

11/23/14 ● FOXBOROUGH
We have returned to the formula.

Win the coin toss. Defer. Exploit a coach who wets himself at the sight of Bill Belichick and Tom Brady. Introduce a player who quit on his old team but is now fully vested in the Patriots way. Completely outsmart the other team in the first half. Do the opposite of what you did offensively last week. Break the opponent's will by managing the clock so that you score on the final play of the first half. Demoralize them in the second half and trigger the celebration over the final 30 minutes of play. Toss in a couple of videoboard shots of the owners in their high chairs and maybe an ad for those $150 Lunar Force 1 kicks. Print the AFC East Champion T-shirts and hats. Sit back and wait for the rave reviews while your fans call talk shows in the spirit of revenge rather than celebration.

Wash. Rinse. Repeat.

The Patriots dismantled the NFC North's first-place Detroit Lions, 34-9, on an unseasonably warm day at Gillette. It was New England's seventh consecutive victory, a span during which the Patriots averaged close to 40 points per game. It was New

England's 14th straight victory over an NFC North team and it improved the Patriots to 32-3 in the second half of all seasons since 2010.

"Our guys did a good job being ready to go," deadpanned Belichick, who benched Jonas Gray, one week after Gray's four-touchdown, 201-yard, Sports Illustrated cover day vs. Indy. Gray overslept and was late for practice Friday. His punishment was right out of the show 'em who's boss, high school playbook. You do it when you know it's not going to hurt you.

The 2014 Patriots are the team we hoped they might be when they acquired Darrelle Revis and Brandon Browner last spring. Their September slump feels like it took place way back during Prohibition. Finally, they have a terrific defense again. Detroit quarterback Matthew Stafford completed only 18 of 46 passes.

The Lions came to Foxborough as possibly the most disrespected first-place opponent in recent history. They owned a 7-3 record and a share of first place in their division, yet they were 7-point underdogs and I could not find a single expert who believed they would win. Belichick, his staff, and his players are too smart to admit the same things, but you know they knew. Detroit had no chance. Jim Caldwell had no chance.

In the mighty jungle that is Gillette in November, the Lions slept all day.

»DAN SHAUGHNESSY

34-9

| DET | 3 | 3 | 0 | 3 |
| NE | 7 | 17 | 3 | 7 |

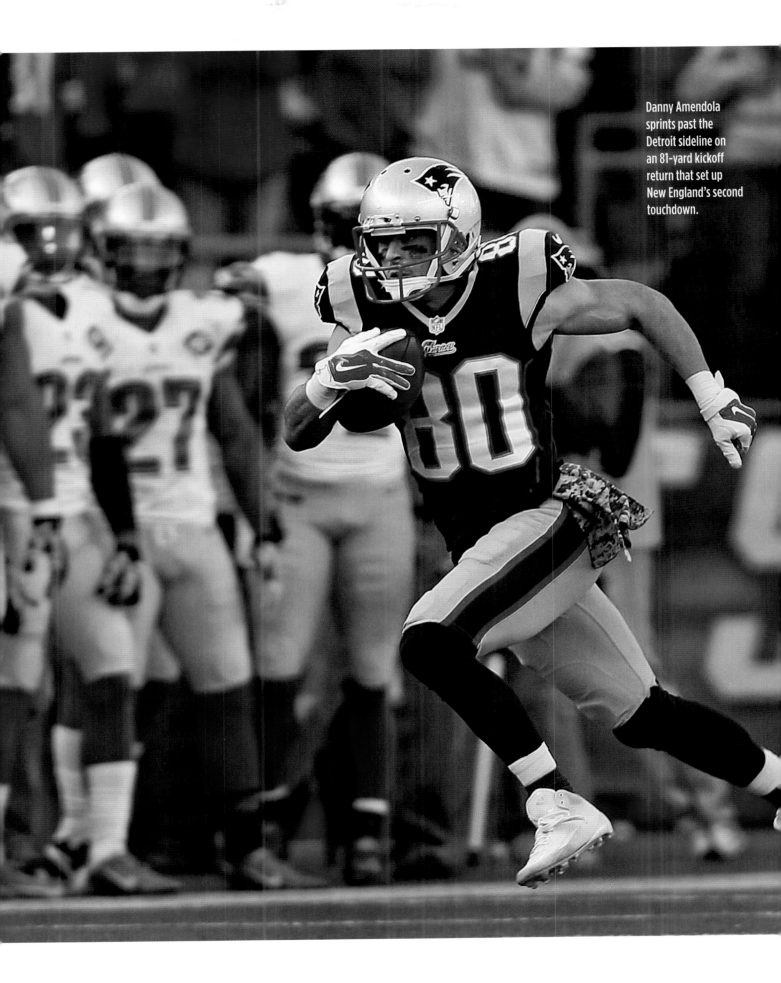

Danny Amendola sprints past the Detroit sideline on an 81-yard kickoff return that set up New England's second touchdown.

11/30/14 ● GREEN BAY

If there is such a thing as a noble, distinguished loss, this was it for the Patriots.

Their seven-game winning streak was kaput, but their Super Bowl contender credentials were intact, perhaps enhanced by what took place on the frozen tundra of Green Bay. The result was negative for Bill Belichick and his team, a 26-21 loss to the Packers before a Lambeau Field record crowd of 78,431, including many Patriots fans who made the pilgrimage to this idyllic football mecca.

But the manner in which it played out provided positive reinforcement. To paraphrase former Arizona Cardinals coach Dennis Green, the 9-3 Patriots are who we thought they were — one of the NFL's elite. So are the 9-3 Packers.

"This was a test for us. It was a big test. I'm sure it was a big test for them, too," said Patriots cornerback Darrelle Revis. "It's two great teams playing. For it to go down to the wire like this, it was expected when you got two great quarterbacks and two great teams going at it. It was a dogfight today."

The Packers came in averaging 43.8 points per game at Lambeau and had scored 30-plus points in all of their previous five home games. The Patriots defense held Aaron Rodgers and the Pack under 30, which is like holding Michael Jordan under 30.

The Patriots were at their bend-but-don't-break best, forcing Green Bay to settle for the Lambeau Leg of Mason Crosby all four times the Packers reached the red zone instead of Lambeau Leap TD celebrations.

Conversely, Tom Brady and the Patriots scored touchdowns on each of their three trips inside the Green Bay 20, which negated the Pack's total yards advantage (478-320).

The Packers punted once all day, with 2:29 left in the third quarter.

The Patriots trailed, 26-21, with 8:35 left. They had gotten a gift, as Green Bay rookie receiver Davante Adams marred a career day (six catches for 121 yards) by dropping a sure touchdown pass on third and 5 from the Patriots 10. Brady drove the Patriots to the Packers 20. He just missed connecting with Rob Gronkowski for the go-ahead score on second down. On third down, he was sacked by Mike Daniels and Mike Neal. Stephen Gostkowski then missed a 47-yard field goal.

Rodgers (24 of 38 for 368 yards and two touchdowns) converted a clutch third-and-4 throw to Randall Cobb.

Game over.

"We played a good football team. That's a good football team," said Belichick. "In the end they made a few more plays than we did."

»CHRISTOPHER L. GASPER

26-21

NE	0	14	0	7
GB	13	10	0	3

Aaron Rodgers completed 24 of 38 passes, including a key late throw for a first down, to end the Patriots' seven-game winning streak.

12/7/14 ☞ SAN DIEGO

Darrelle Revis wore a big smile as the final seconds ticked down. He turned toward the pro-Patriots crowd behind his bench, and encouraged them with hand gestures to bring him the love.

Revis, and the rest of his defensive teammates, deserved every bit of glory.

The Patriots' defense brought the thunder on a night when Tom Brady and the offense struggled to hold up their end of the bargain. They pounded the Chargers into submission, stifling Philip Rivers and leaving his teammates battered and their egos bruised.

The Patriots allowed a season-low 216 yards and only 7 points — San Diego's other 7 came when Darrell Stuckey returned a Brandon LaFell fumble for a touchdown. In the second half, they allowed just 100 yards and didn't give up a point. They held Rivers to just 189 yards passing and sacked him four times. They intercepted Rivers once, and should have had a pick-six if not for a highly questionable penalty on Brandon Browner for hitting a defenseless receiver.

To go on the road and shut down the league's No. 7-ranked passing attack, led by an annual Pro Bowler in Rivers, was one of the more impressive feats by the Patriots all season, on either side of the ball. Brady doesn't have to carry the team on his back anymore. Now, finally, the Patriots have a defense that can carry Brady.

The Patriots struggled offensively in the third quarter, going three-and-out on their first four possessions. They began making progress as the fourth began, putting a field goal on the board to reclaim the lead at 16-14, their first since taking a 3-0 lead in the first quarter. Julian Edelman sealed the win with a 69-yard catch-and-run in the fourth quarter, outrunning the defense for his third touchdown of the season.

"Great play," Brady said. "We found a little spot to throw it and Julian made a great catch and run. We needed that type of play at that time of the game, and the defense took over from there."

As the final seconds clicked down, Revis stayed on the sideline while his teammates convened at midfield for handshakes. He danced around the bench area with a huge smile on his face and one finger pointed in the air.

The Patriots looked like the No. 1 team in the AFC, and it was the defense that was carrying them there.

»BEN VOLIN

23-14

NE	3	10	0	10
SD	0	14	0	0

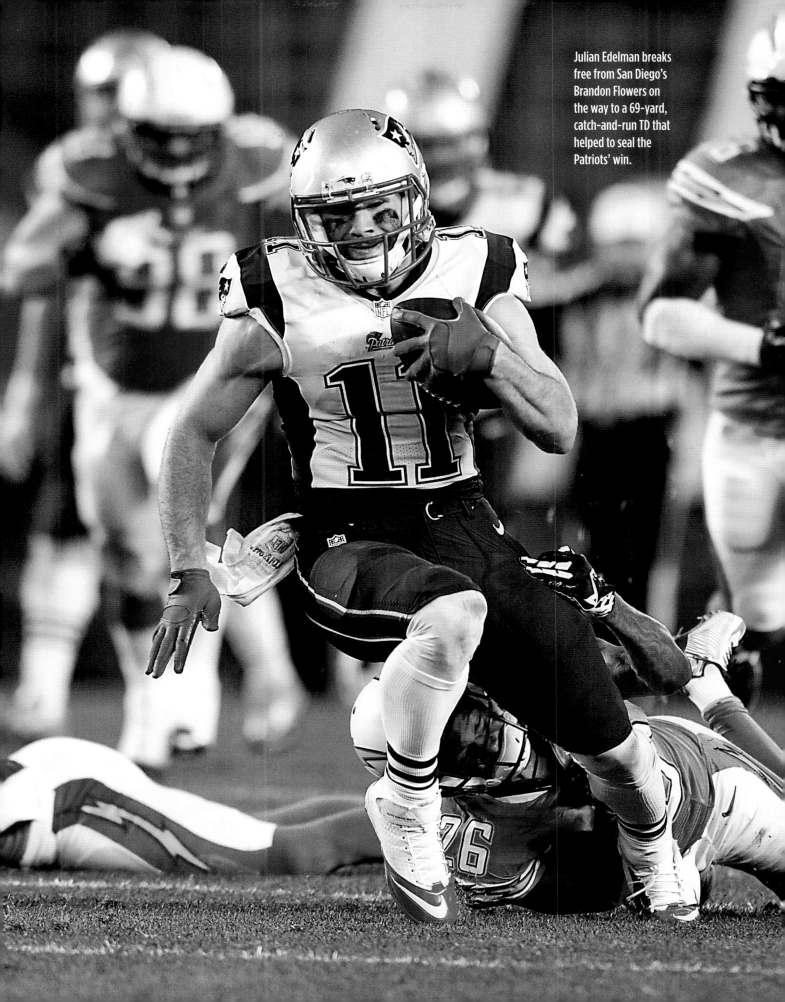

Julian Edelman breaks free from San Diego's Brandon Flowers on the way to a 69-yard, catch-and-run TD that helped to seal the Patriots' win.

12/14/14 ● FOXBOROUGH

The Patriots came out of the locker room for the second half against the Dolphins looking little like the lackluster team they were in the first half. They turned a 14-13 halftime lead into a rout in the third quarter, clinching their sixth consecutive AFC East title with a 41-13 win at Gillette Stadium.

It is the 12th division title of the Bill Belichick era; no coach has won more division crowns since the NFL/AFL merger. Belichick came into the game tied at 11 with Hall of Famer Don Shula.

The Patriots scored a franchise-record 24 third-quarter points, and scored 27 second-half points while shutting out the Dolphins, using great starting field position on two possessions to their best advantage.

Although Miami had defeated the Patriots on its field in the regular-season opener, this game proved to be another reminder that the Dolphins aren't ready to dethrone the Patriots.

Tom Brady and the offense quickly established in the second half that there would not be a repeat of Week 1. The Patriots got the ball to start the third, and opened with a 34-yard pass from Brady (21 of 35, 287 yards, 2 touchdowns, 1 interception) to Rob Gronkowski.

Later, facing third and 11, Brady dropped back, scanned the field, pump-faked, and took off running, not stopping until he was knocked out of bounds 17 yards later by Dolphins safety Walt Aikens. It was Brady's longest run since 2007.

Brady said he was "pissed off" during the play, which is why he didn't slide.

"I could have slid, but I wasn't in the best mood at that time," he said.

LeGarrette Blount scored immediately after Brady's run, crossing the goal line from 3 yards out.

Miami opened the second half with a punt, and the Patriots increased their lead to 24-13 with a Stephen Gostkowski field goal. It made Gostkowski the franchise's all-time leader in scoring, passing Adam Vinatieri.

Two plays, in rapid succession, effectively put the game out of reach. Miami's Ryan Tannehill was picked off on first down as Patrick Chung pulled in a ball intended for running back Lamar Miller that he had batted up in the air. One snap later, Brady hit Gronkowski down the left seam for a 27-yard touchdown that put the Patriots ahead, 31-13.

Then a short Brandon Fields punt combined with a 13-yard Danny Amendola return gave the Patriots good field position once again, and they turned it into a touchdown, Brady with a perfect floater to Julian Edelman for a 6-yard score.

»SHALISE MANZA YOUNG

41-13

MIA	3	10	0	0
NE	7	7	24	3

Tom Brady salutes Julian Edelman after a 6-yard TD hookup that gave the Patriots a team-record 24 points in the third quarter and a 38-13 lead.

DOLPHINS
VIKINGS
RAIDERS
CHIEFS
BENGALS
BILLS
JETS
BEARS
BRONCOS
COLTS
LIONS
PACKERS
CHARGERS
DOLPHINS
JETS
BILLS

12/21/14 ● E. RUTHERFORD, NJ
The large right hand of Vince Wilfork helped save the Patriots from the embarrassment of losing to the three-win Jets, the uncertainty of not clinching a first-round bye in the playoffs, and the possibility of losing the AFC's top seed. Wilfork made contact with Nick Folk's 52-yard fourth-quarter field-goal try, a kick that could have given the Jets the lead with just more than five minutes to play in a game in which points were at an absolute premium.

The attempt was well short, teammates crowded around Wilfork, the Patriots' sideline celebrated, and a few minutes later the offense got the first down it needed to kill the clock and preserve a 17-16 victory over a division rival.

The victory ensured the Patriots would have one of the first two seeds in the AFC, and the first-round bye that comes with it.

"I had a good opportunity to make a play and I did it for the team," said Wilfork. "It was nothing special that I did. I penetrated a little bit and got my hands up and got a piece of it.

I'm glad it helped my team win a ballgame. That's what it's all about."

In both Patriots wins over the Jets this season — by a combined 3 points — a blocked kick played a significant role. In October, Chris Jones blocked Folk's last-second attempt to give New York the win at Gillette Stadium.

Devin McCourty believes it is the defense's job to come up with key plays at key times.

"That's our job description," he said. "We have enough talent that we feel we can go out there and do that in big games; in every game, really."

An interception by Jamie Collins in the third quarter put the Patriots inside Jets' territory, helping set up the go-ahead touchdown.

The possession was punctuated by another Brady scramble, this one for 11 yards. Jonas Gray, whose touches increased with LeGarrette Blount unable to play, punched it in from a yard.

The offense was once again flat early. The first quarter saw seven total possessions and seven punts. Brady (23 of 35, 182 yards, touchdown, interception) was sacked four times in the first half.

The Patriots trailed, 10-7, at the half and 13-7 with 6:39 to play in the third quarter before mounting their comeback, first with a short field goal from Stephen Gostkowski and then the touchdown in the fourth quarter.

"That was great," Brady said of coming from behind. "I'm glad it came out the way it did, it makes for a better Christmas."

»SHALISE MANZA YOUNG

17-16

NE	0	7	3	7
NYJ	0	10	3	3

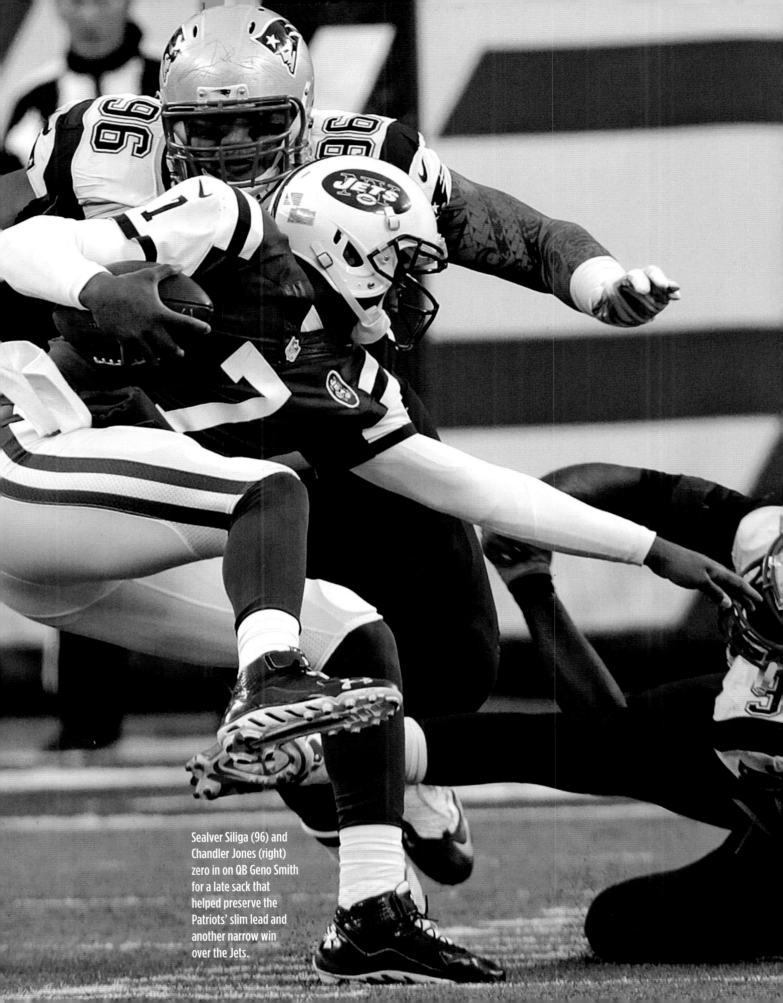

Sealver Siliga (96) and Chandler Jones (right) zero in on QB Geno Smith for a late sack that helped preserve the Patriots' slim lead and another narrow win over the Jets.

DOLPHINS
VIKINGS
RAIDERS
CHIEFS
BENGALS
BILLS
JETS
BEARS
BRONCOS
COLTS
LIONS
PACKERS
CHARGERS
DOLPHINS
JETS
BILLS

12/28/14 ☞ FOXBOROUGH
The Patriots won. In blowout fashion, even.

No, not on the scoreboard. Officially, they lost to Buffalo, 17-9, the Bills' first win in Foxborough since 2000. That was Bill Belichick's first season with the Patriots and pre-dates Gillette Stadium, which opened in 2002.

But the score didn't matter. The Patriots already had locked up the No. 1 seed, a first-round bye, and home-field advantage throughout the AFC playoffs before opening kickoff.

Only two things mattered in this game: staying healthy and getting the backups some much-needed work. And the Patriots aced the test on both fronts.

Belichick wasn't taking any chances, perhaps spooked by Wes Welker's torn ACL in the 2009 regular-season finale. He sat Rob Gronkowski, who was healthy for an entire regular season for the first time since 2011. Now we'll finally know how dangerous the Patriots can be in the playoffs with a healthy Gronk.

The coach sat any player who had even the faintest injury: Dont'a Hightower and his shoulder injury, even though he played last week; Julian Edelman and the concussion he suffered two weeks ago; Dan Connolly and the knee injury he suffered two weeks ago; Jonas Gray and the sprained ankle he suffered last week, even though he was able to later return to that game; Brandon Browner and the groin injury he suffered in practice last week; Sebastian Vollmer and the back injury he suffered in Friday's practice.

Kyle Arrington was active and in uniform in case of emergency, but he missed last week's game with a hamstring injury and was the only active Patriots player not to enter the final game of the season.

And many of those who did play — including Tom Brady, Darrelle Revis, and Chandler Jones — came out after halftime.

"We have some guys that have played a lot of football for us, and we felt like today would be an opportunity for us to have some guys who haven't played as much to get an opportunity to play," Belichick said afterward. "That's kind of the way we managed the team. We tried to create opportunities for some guys that the experience I think will benefit them going forward."

Week 17 was about perspective. Keep Gronk and the superstars healthy? Check. Get some reps for the backups? Check. Win the game? That wasn't very high on the list of priorities.

»BEN VOLIN

17-9

BUF	7	10	0	0
NE	3	3	3	0

Reserve QB Jimmy Garoppolo bears the brunt of the Bills' defense as the Patriot starters rested for much of the meaningless season finale.

»FROM 65 · The offensive line finally clicked. Rob Gronkowski got healthy. Brady got more comfortable in the pocket. They did what Belichick drills into their heads every day: They just continued to do their job. And then, bang — a 26-point win against Cincinnati. A 28-point shellacking of the Chicago Bears, followed by a 22-point beatdown of the Denver Broncos. Seven wins in a row, by an average margin of 20 points, en route to a 12-4 regular season record.

"There's definitely times where you're kind of back against the wall and you've got to show a lot of mental toughness and a lot of fight," Brady said. "The best teams that I've been around have been the most mentally and physically tough teams, and anything that can challenge those and strengthen those definitely ends up being a positive."

FIGU

'IT WAS THE RIGHT DECISION TO MAKE. DOESN'T MEAN IT DIDN'T HURT, BUT HISTORY HAS SHOWN IT WAS RIGHT.'

DREW BLEDSOE · ON LOSING HIS JOB TO TOM BRADY IN 2001

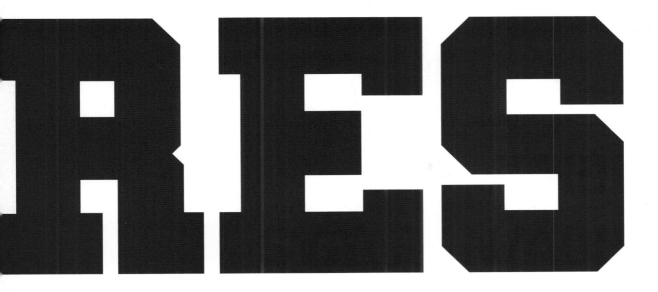

BY JOHN POWERS / Globe Staff

In the NFL, where parity is the orchestrated objective, dynasties aren't calculated so much by championships won as by appearances in the title game and in the playoffs. By that standard, five franchises have stood out during the past half-century: the Green Bay Packers, Pittsburgh Steelers, Dallas Cowboys, San Francisco 49ers, and the Patriots. » Since 1960 that quintet has won a combined 27 NFL crowns, played for the championship 39 times, and competed in the postseason 128 times. What sets the Patriots apart is that they've consistently made it to January in an age of free agency and a salary cap that make for annual roster churn. » "They've clearly figured out how to deal with continuity in the discontinuity era," observed Steve Young, who earned three Super Bowl rings with the 49ers. Since 2001, New England has reached the title game six times, winning four, and qualified for postseason play 12 times. "The Patriots don't win it every year, but they're around it every year." » It's no coincidence that since 2001, they've had the same owner, same coach, and same quarterback. That stability of identity, of philosophy, and of expectation is why free agents such as Darrelle Revis opt to compete for a franchise that expects no less than to play for a Super Bowl. "You've got to love the pressure and live for the pressure to play in New England," said Tedy Bruschi, who got to the playoffs nine times during his 13 seasons. "That's the way it is."

01.26.1986
Louisiana
Superdome
New Orleans,
Louisiana

SUPER

46-10

| CHI | 13 | 10 | 21 | 2 |
| NE | 3 | 0 | 0 | 7 |

The wild-card Patriots reached their first Super Bowl by winning three road playoff games, capped by their 31-14, "Squish the Fish" victory over the Dolphins for the AFC title. The magical run was ended disastrously by the 15-1 Bears, who boasted one of the dominant defenses in NFL history. Chicago manhandled the Pats, recording as many sacks (7, including this one of Pats' QB Steve Grogan by Otis Wilson) as rushing yards allowed (7 yards on 11 carries).

BOWLS

01.26.1997
Louisiana
Superdome
New Orleans,
Louisiana

The Patriots were mostly held in check by a Green Bay defense that sacked Drew Bledsoe (11) five times and picked off four of his passes. Brett Favre threw for two scores and ran for another as the Packers built a 27-14 halftime lead. New England closed to within 27-21 late in the third quarter on a Curtis Martin touchdown run, but game MVP Desmond Howard returned the ensuing kickoff 99 yards to dash the Patriots' comeback hopes.

35-21

GB	10	17	8	0
NE	14	0	7	0

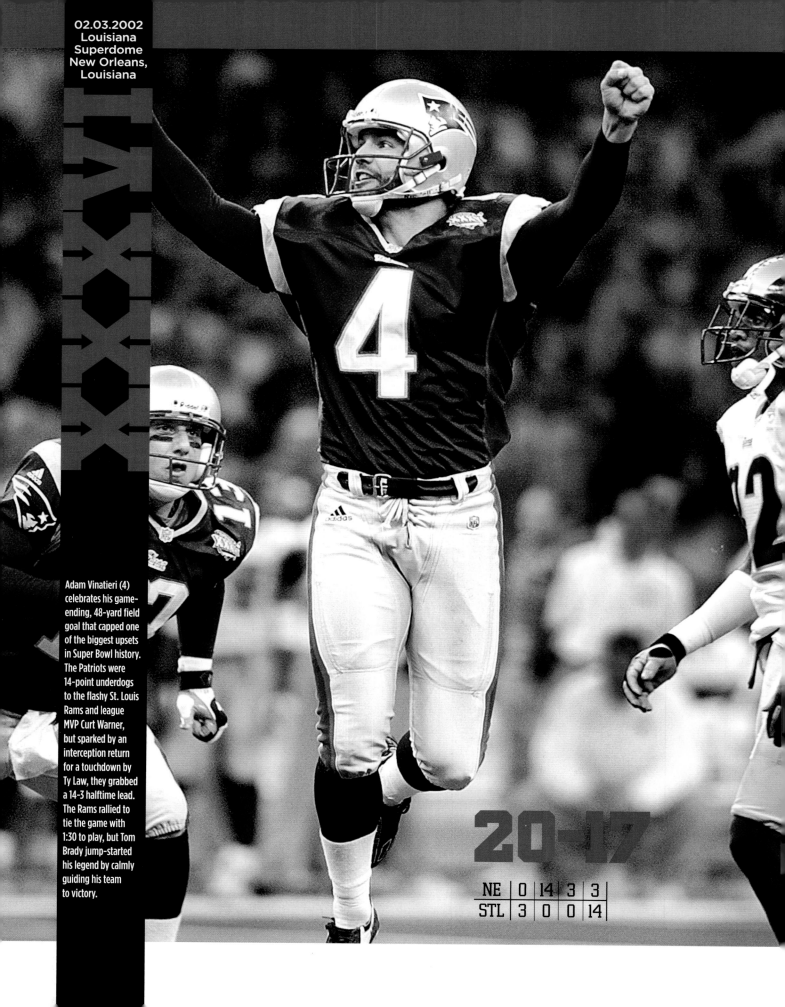

XXXVI

Adam Vinatieri (4) celebrates his game-ending, 48-yard field goal that capped one of the biggest upsets in Super Bowl history. The Patriots were 14-point underdogs to the flashy St. Louis Rams and league MVP Curt Warner, but sparked by an interception return for a touchdown by Ty Law, they grabbed a 14-3 halftime lead. The Rams rallied to tie the game with 1:30 to play, but Tom Brady jump-started his legend by calmly guiding his team to victory.

20-17

NE	0	14	3	3
STL	3	0	0	14

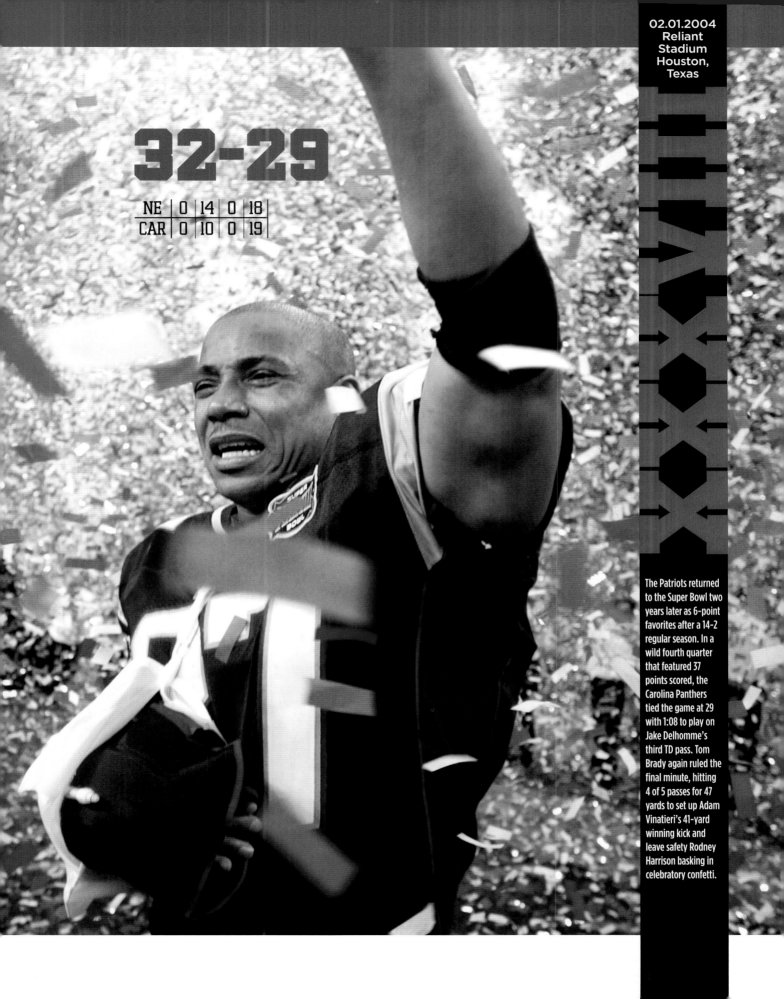

32-29

NE	0	14	0	18
CAR	0	10	0	19

The Patriots returned to the Super Bowl two years later as 6-point favorites after a 14-2 regular season. In a wild fourth quarter that featured 37 points scored, the Carolina Panthers tied the game at 29 with 1:08 to play on Jake Delhomme's third TD pass. Tom Brady again ruled the final minute, hitting 4 of 5 passes for 47 yards to set up Adam Vinatieri's 41-yard winning kick and leave safety Rodney Harrison basking in celebratory confetti.

02.06.2005
Alltel
Stadium
Jacksonville,
Florida

XXXIX

24-21

NE	0	7	7	10
PHI	0	7	7	7

After another 14-2 regular season, the Patriots joined the Dallas Cowboys as the only two franchises to win three Super Bowls in four years. For the first time, the Super Bowl was tied entering the final quarter, but Tom Brady (12) drove the Patriots 66 yards to a touchdown, then to a field goal. The Eagles closed within three points, but their hopes evaporated when Rodney Harrison picked off Donovan McNabb's desperate pass, one of four Philadelphia turnovers.

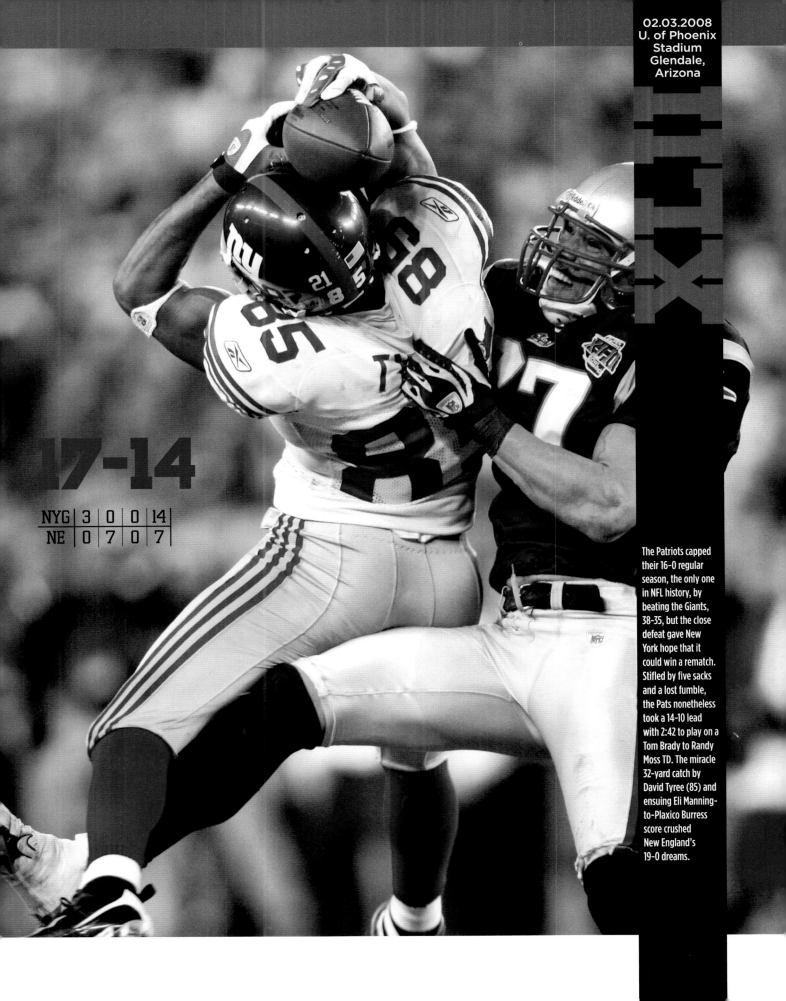

17-14

NYG	3	0	0	14
NE	0	7	0	7

The Patriots capped their 16-0 regular season, the only one in NFL history, by beating the Giants, 38-35, but the close defeat gave New York hope that it could win a rematch. Stifled by five sacks and a lost fumble, the Pats nonetheless took a 14-10 lead with 2:42 to play on a Tom Brady to Randy Moss TD. The miracle 32-yard catch by David Tyree (85) and ensuing Eli Manning-to-Plaxico Burress score crushed New England's 19-0 dreams.

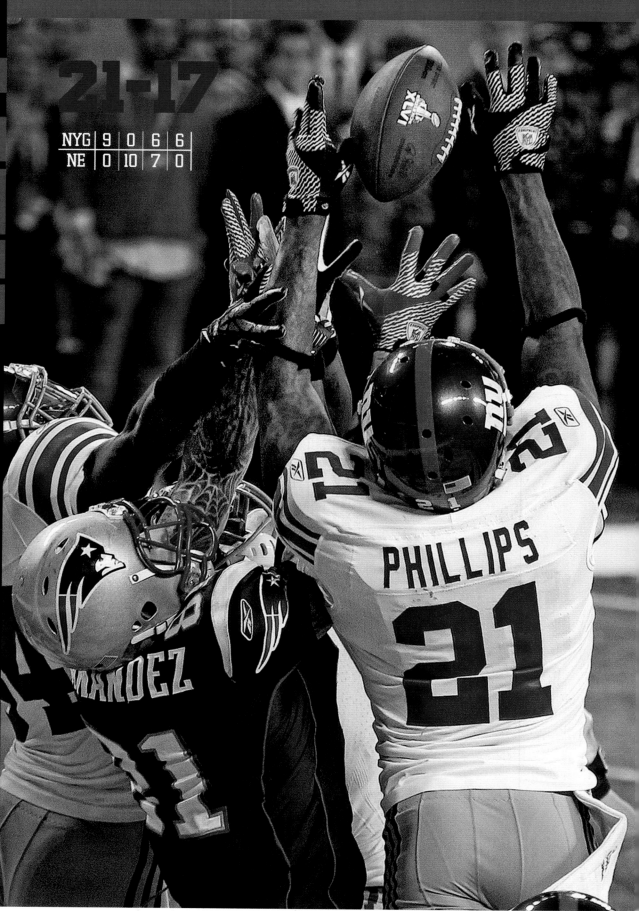

XLVI

21-17

NYG	9	0	6	6
NE	0	10	7	0

The 13-3 Patriots edged Baltimore, 23-20, for the AFC title to set up a rematch with the 9-7 New York Giants and Eli Manning. New England led, 17-9, after Tom Brady hit Aaron Hernandez for a 12-yard score, but the Giants scored the game's final 12 points on two field goals and Ahmad Bradshaw's 6-yard run with 57 seconds left. The final drive was aided by a dramatic catch, by Mario Manningham, and a crucial drop by the Patriots' Wes Welker three plays earlier.

02.01.2015
U. of Phoenix
Stadium
Glendale,
Arizona

XLIX

Malcolm Butler (21) instantly entered Boston sports lore when he jumped the Seahawks' goal-line route for an interception of Russell Wilson that saved the Patriots' 28-24 victory over Seattle with 20 seconds to play. Tom Brady, who completed a Super Bowl-record 37 passes for four TDs, was the MVP for a third time as the Pats rallied from 10 points down in the final quarter. Julian Edelman tallied the game's final points on a 3-yard touchdown catch with 2:02 to play.

28-24

NE	0	14	0	14
SEA	0	14	10	0

Make room for one more banner. Including playoffs the Patriots are 101-19 at home since Gillette Stadium opened in 2002. Their regular season record at home is 88-16.

COACH
BELICHICK

In private moments, when no one is around, Bill Belichick must light up the occasional victory cigar.

Belichick is the son Red Auerbach never had.

After the Patriots' epic Divisional Round victory, Baltimore Ravens coach John Harbaugh complained about New England's inventive offensive formation, making reference to "a trick type of thing," and "the deception part of it." Harbaugh also said, "It's not something that anybody's ever done before."

Not something that anybody's ever done before. Like when Red would run his team into shape before the start of every season so the Celtics would start fast while other teams were running themselves into game shape during the regular season; like when Red played fast-break basketball while other teams were standing still.

Playing chess while the others are playing checkers. That always was the way with Red Auerbach. And that's Bill Belichick. If you are the other team, Bill gets in your head. Like Red.

Celtics rival Pat Riley spent many hours fretting about Red turning up the heat in the Old Boston Garden. Riley also was convinced Red had somebody

pulling fire alarms at the Lakers' hotel headquarters when they stayed in Boston.

"I thought [Auerbach] was the man behind everything," Riley said. "When you're in that situation, it becomes more and more of a hate."

Red loved it. Told that his opponents were convinced he was playing dirty, Red would fold his arms across his chest, sit back in his chair, and take a puff of a Hoyo de Monterrey. The mere inference that he was screwing with rivals took his opponents' eyes off the job at hand.

Our Billy is the master of deception. Who will ever forget that night in Denver in 2003, when the Patriots appeared beaten until Belichick ordered Lonie Paxton to snap the ball out of the end zone on fourth and 10 from their 1-yard line while trailing, 24-23, with three minutes left? The intentional safety put the Patriots in position to win. And they did, 30-26.

"I really don't know what to say," Denver coach Mike Shanahan stuttered after the game.

Something nobody has ever done before.

Bill Belichick and Red

Auerbach. They are brothers of the whistle and clipboard. And it's more than just being smarter than everybody else and winning the mind games.

Like Bill, Red was ever-angry at the league office. He thought the league bosses had it in for the Celtics.

Red and Bill were/are socially awkward and totally ungracious in defeat. Think Belichick has had some frosty postgame handshakes? Red once punched the owner of the St. Louis Hawks before a playoff game.

Like Red, Bill would trade a family member if it would help him win.

Red won nine NBA championships as a coach and another seven as a GM; he held all the coaching records when he retired from the bench in 1966. No coach has more NFL playoff wins than Belichick, who is tied with Don Shula for most Super Bowl appearances (six) and has as many Lombardi trophies (four) as Chuck Noll.

When it comes to the Genius of Bill, we have moved into immortality. Belichick is so good he has even mastered the coin toss.

Red would have loved this guy.

DAN SHAUGHNESSY • *Globe Staff*

QUARTERBACK
BRADY

Tom Brady had come full circle. At age 37, he was right back where he began his NFL career — having his ability doubted.

Brady was no longer a scrawny, anonymous sixth-round pick. He was one of the greatest quarterbacks in NFL history, a two-time league MVP and a three-time Super Bowl winner.

His name had become synonymous with superlative quarterback play and dashing style. But doubt is doubt, and even with a list of accomplishments longer than "War and Peace," Brady is still fueled by those doubts.

The great debate of the Patriots' 2014 offseason was whether Brady, about to enter his 15th NFL season, was a deity in decline. Whether the ravages of time and NFL defenders with malevolent intentions had taken their toll on TB12.

Proponents of the decline theory pointed to Brady's numbers from last season as evidence. He completed 60.5 percent of his passes, his lowest since 2003. He was sacked 40 times, the most since 2001. He threw 25 touchdown passes, his lowest number since 2006, when his wide receivers created less

separation than a pair of hands folded in prayer.

The official Declaration of Brady Declination came from Pro Football Focus in June. The website committed heresy, making the case with in-depth statistical analysis that Brady was no longer among the top five quarterbacks in the NFL.

He was faltering when pressured and losing some of his trademark composure in the pocket when forced to hold the ball, never mind that he had been asked to tutor rookie wideouts and only had tight end Rob Gronkowski for seven games.

Brady has always tended to internalize slights, whether they came as the backup quarterback on the freshman team at Junipero Serra High School, as a time-share quarterback at the University of Michigan, from NFL Draft scouting reports, or media pundits more recently.

"Those things end up making up your character," said Brady back in September. "You can always tap into those things when you've got to dig deep to see what you're all about and use those things as a way to motivate you and to inspire you to do better.

"I use everything I can get

to motivate me. Yeah, I do internalize things, and yeah, those things come out when it matters. The ultimate goal is winning, and it's team wins. That's always been my best tool to motivate me. If you're not in here to win, you won't be in the NFL very long."

Does the veteran quarterback ever watch film and see a throw he would have made or a hit he would have avoided were he in his late 20s, not his late 30s?

Brady paused at the question, like he was surveying a defense.

"Um ... you know it's, I don't really kind of compare it like that," he said. "I don't know. That's for other people to judge. I feel like I'm trying to go out there and be the best I can be. Things that I used to do, or things that I can do now, I don't think about those things. Those don't really come into my mind.

"Hopefully, I just keep getting better. That's what I'm hoping I do. Whether I do or not, that's for other people to judge. That's not really how I gain my satisfaction."

The truth is Brady is never satisfied. It is what makes him great. He is always chasing ghosts of greatness, real and imagined.

CHRISTOPHER L. GASPER • *Globe Staff*

12

CORNERBACK
REVIS

Darrelle Revis has been a Patriot for a full season, and the perception about him around here is still all wrong.

Not the perception about him on the field, of course. He came here with a reputation of being one of the best cornerbacks in the league, and he has lived up to every outsized expectation.

It's about what Revis is really like on the inside. There's a misperception about what makes him tick.

Anyone who follows the NFL knows Revis likes to get paid. Some of Revis's most memorable moments include him holding out of training camp with the Jets as a rookie in 2007, holding out again in 2010, and the massive contract he signed with Tampa Bay two years ago worth $16 million per season.

But don't mistake business savvy with greed. He hates the "mercenary" label. His friends and confidants quickly point out that Revis never missed a regular-season snap because of a contract holdout.

You can call him "Me-vis" or "Revi$" if you want, but money isn't why he signed with the Patriots in March after the Buccaneers cut him.

Revis's camp first approached the Jets about a reunion, and after being spurned, Revis turned to the Patriots and quickly signed on the dotted line for one year and $12 million (with a team option to extend to two years and $32 million). At 29, Revis was hungry for a ring and starting to think about legacy. He went to two AFC Championship games with the Jets, but hadn't been on the NFL's biggest stage.

Revis likes playing for Bill Belichick. He likes the Patriots' no-nonsense approach and professional environment. He likes the guys in the locker room. He likes competing for Super Bowls.

"It's been everything he thought it would be," a source close to Revis said, "and more."

The Patriots, of course, love having Revis, too. They love that he can hang with the top receivers in the NFL; that he allows them to be more creative with the other 10 players on defense; that other than one tardiness in October, he has shown up to work every day and brings the same intensity to the practice field that he does on game days.

"He's one of the most competitive guys I've been

around at that position," Tom Brady said. "I mean, he hates when you catch a ball on him. He's had a big challenge covering a lot of the premier players that we faced this year, every week he gets a tough assignment, and he always seems to do a great job."

They love that, as fellow cornerback Kyle Arrington put it, "nobody's harder on him than himself."

"Sometimes we'll just be sitting in the locker room, ... and his iPad's on and he'll be cussing himself, and I'm like, 'What's wrong with you? Something happen?'" Arrington said. "And he's looking at film from a previous week, where he can make corrections. That's the kind of guy he is."

Revis has been a great culture fit, because he didn't have to be taught the "Patriot Way." He was already a Belichick-type player before he arrived in New England.

"Like I tell people all the time, the 'Patriot Way' is simple," safety Devin McCourty said. "Just be professional, do the right thing, show up on time, practice hard. And I think that's what he already was."

BEN VOLIN • *Globe Staff*

24

DEFENSIVE END
NINKOVICH

Disinterested, disgruntled, and on one memorable occasion completely disgusted, Rob Ninkovich had every intention of quitting.

Ninkovich, then a teenaged eighth-grader in the Chicago suburb of New Lenox, Ill., exceeded the youth football weight limit, so he decided to give wrestling a try. He hated it from the start. As a 180-pound heavyweight, Ninkovich was paired against bigger, more experienced wrestlers. The worst was when he hit the mat after another wrestler in a prior match had vomited.

So Ninkovich, as teens sometimes do, complained to his parents. Mike and Deborah Ninkovich, as sensible, responsible parents often do, delivered an answer the teen didn't exactly appreciate.

"I came home and said, 'Dad, I don't like this.' And he says, 'Well, you're going to have to see it through,' so I had to finish the whole thing," Ninkovich said. "I got better as I went along, but it wasn't my thing. Longest year of my athletic life. I wanted to quit after the first day."

Only he didn't. It wouldn't be the last time the future NFL defensive end chose not to quit, and the Patriots are better for

it. Because of the lesson handed down years ago to Ninkovich – the son of an iron worker, and the grandson of an iron worker – he knew that when life appears to take an unsavory turn, something sweet might be waiting right around the corner. He's seen it in his professional life, and his personal one.

Before Rob Ninkovich became the player he is now, he was a senior at Lincoln-Way Central High School with no college scholarship offers. After spending two years at nearby Joliet (Ill.) Junior College, he went on to play at Purdue.

"He may not be the most athletic guy they've got, but he'll outwork you, he's smarter, and he'll do things the way you coach him, while others might say, 'I'm going to do it my way.' Robbie only wants to get better," said Tom Minnick, who recruited Ninkovich to Joliet and is now the head coach at Arizona Western College. "His goal was to play in the NFL, like a lot of kids, but he took advantage of it. I knew he'd be successful, because he didn't do everything you asked him to do. He did more."

In 2006, as the fifth round of the NFL Draft was beginning, Ninkovich thought he'd be

selected by the Patriots, who had the 136th overall pick. Instead, he went No. 135, to the New Orleans Saints.

"My mom asked me, 'Where do you not want to go play?' I said New Orleans. Hurricane Katrina had just hit," Ninkovich said. "I love New Orleans now."

That's primarily because he met his wife Paige while briefly playing for the Saints. The couple has an 18-month-old daughter, Olivia.

Ninkovich is humble but has always been extremely confident. He's stubborn but responds best when coached by old-school, military-type (his words), strong individuals (sound like anyone in particular, perhaps favors a hoodie?). He's quiet, but not afraid to speak up.

"I'm stubborn. I would say it's helped me get to where I'm at, because I was persistent, and being stubborn helped me forget about things that could have kept me out of the league," Ninkovich said. "I think that goes back to having confidence in yourself. I was always confident that I could get to a high level and play at a high level. I just needed the right chance, the right opportunity. Life's all about opportunity."

MICHAEL WHITMER • *Globe Staff*

50

TIGHT END
GRONKOWSKI

The Patriots' offense looks completely different when a healthy Rob Gronkowski lines up at tight end.

Tom Brady does a good job conducting the offense, but Rob Gronkowski makes it sing.

Gronkowski can open up holes in the run game. His mere presence can make it easier for Julian Edelman to find open space downfield. Knowing he'll be on the field can lead to sleepless nights for defensive coordinators.

This is not super-sizing his impact to match his super-sized frame. Gronkowski is just that good.

"He changes everything," says Greg Cosell, executive producer of "NFL Matchup" and a man who watches more NFL and college game film than nearly anyone on the planet.

At 6 feet, 6 inches, a playing weight near 270 pounds, an obsession with the weight room, and a ridiculously low body-fat percentage, Gronkowski has long looked like a chiseled gridiron action

hero. But after seven surgeries in less than 24 months, on his ankle, forearm, back, and most recently on his right anterior cruciate ligament, Gronkowski is borderline bionic.

Perhaps it's fitting though, given that he can do for the Patriots' offense what no human not named Brady can.

"In the pass game he changes everything because of what he dictates from a coverage standpoint. He changes everything in the run game, too, because he's a good blocker," says Cosell. "Linebackers aren't fast enough to keep up with him and he's so much bigger than safeties. He's 270 and he moves really, really well. How are you going to defend Gronkowski and have bodies available in run defense?"

An AFC source offered more on what makes Gronkowski so valuable.

"When he's not out there, they don't have a tight end. I don't care who they put out there, when he's not there,

they don't have a tight end," the source said. "If you put someone in there that's not him, [defenses] are not worried about that tight end running a 2-yard drag or a quick outlet, but when Gronk is out there, they're worried.

"You have to be disciplined — is it pass or run? If it's run, he's a darn good blocker. If it's pass, he can run all the routes, so defensively you're going to have to double-team him, the D-end has to get a hand on him, which slows his pass rush. The linebacker has to be strong in coverage, and if it's a safety, he's going to beat him with his size or his speed. If you put a corner on him, Brady is smart enough to check to a run.

"He and Brady make the offense go for everyone else. Gronk can get Edelman open, he can get [Danny] Amendola open. Based on the formation, based on the play, he can get those guys open. When he's on the field, he's a difference-maker."

SHALISE MANZA YOUNG • *Globe Staff*

87

WIDE RECEIVER
EDELMAN

Whether he's behind the wheel of a pace car at a NASCAR race, as he was last summer at New Hampshire Motor Speedway, or tracking a Tom Brady throw, or settling beneath a sky-scraping punt, Julian Edelman has always cut a dashing figure for the Patriots.

The versatility Edelman has displayed in his NFL career, returning kicks, covering kicks, playing slot receiver, outside receiver, slot defender — in short, all the positions he never played at Kent State, where as a senior dual-threat quarterback in 2008 he amassed a career-high 3,190 yards total offense — earned him a handsome four-year contract extension in March worth a reported $19 million, including a $17 million base ($8 million guaranteed).

"You know, I've been here a couple of years and I've never really worried about that kind of stuff," Edelman said, referring to the whopping raise he earned over the one-year, $715,000 contract he signed last offseason as an unrestricted free agent.

"As you know, it's an unpredictable business, and I'm just trying to go out there in my role and do what I can to improve every day."

Even when it means returning punts?

"I love returning punts," said Edelman, the 2009 seventh-round draft choice (232d overall) who set a franchise record with his 94-yard punt return for a touchdown at Miami Jan. 2, 2011, and for single-season punt return average (15.5) in 2012. "That's a part of the game that gave me the opportunity to make this team."

Last season, Edelman broke 1,000 receiving yards for the first time in his career, leading the Patriots with 105 receptions for 1,056 yards (10.1 average) and six touchdowns. There's little wonder then that Edelman came to camp with a bounce in his step as he entered his sixth season with the Patriots. His breakout season was capped just before the start of camp by the thrilling experience of serving as the pace car driver at NHMS, where pole-sitter Kyle Busch playfully bumped Edelman from behind during the pace lap.

"It was good to help me actually set the pace for what our times were on our conditioning runs," Edelman joked. "It was a fun experience and I appreciated it. You get an appreciation for that sport when you see it up close."

Upon closer inspection, Edelman's NFL experience has been replete with several challenges, including the adjustment to all the new positions he never played in college. But the toughest? It wasn't serving as Wes Welker's understudy early on his career. It was, simply, a matter of gaining Brady's trust.

"It's pretty tough, I'm not going to lie," Edelman said. "When you've played with a guy for so long and have been in the same system and have played with a lot of phenomenal players, a lot of great players in the past, he's expecting a lot because he's seen it done, so, you know, it's tough."

Once Brady's trust is earned, it can never be taken for granted, Edelman has learned.

"The way you earn his trust is just going out there and being consistent and always improving, seeing what he's seeing and being on the same page," Edelman said. "Confidence is built through execution and in practice when you do it consistently. So when you're out there consistently doing the right assignment, making a play, and doing what you have to do at a high rate, that's when you can go out and play your fastest and play with the utmost of confidence."

MICHAEL VEGA • *Globe Staff*

NEW ENGLAND

Danny **AMENDOLA** | WR
80 Texas Tech
5'11 | 195 lbs | exp. 6

LeGarrette **BLOUNT** | RB
29 Oregon
6'0 | 250 lbs | exp. 5

Tom **BRADY** | QB
12 Michigan
6'4 | 225 lbs | exp. 15

Dan **CONNOLLY** | LG
63 Southeast Missouri State
6'4 | 305 lbs | exp. 9

Julian **EDELMAN** | WR
11 Kent State
5'10 | 200 lbs | exp. 6

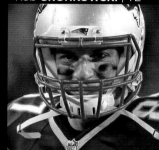

Rob **GRONKOWSKI** | TE
87 Arizona
6'6 | 265 lbs | exp. 5

Michael **HOOMANAWANUI** | TE
47 Illinois
6'4 | 260 lbs | exp. 5

Brandon **LaFELL** | WR
19 LSU
6'3 | 210 lbs | exp. 5

Matthew **SLATER** | WR
18 UCLA
6'0 | 210 lbs | exp. 7

Nate **SOLDER** | LT
77 Colorado
6'8 | 320 lbs | exp. 4

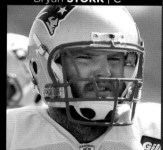

Bryan **STORK** | C
66 Florida State
6'4 | 310 lbs | exp. R

Shane **VEREEN** | RB
34 California
5'10 | 205 lbs | exp. 4

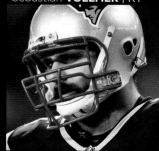

Sebastian **VOLLMER** | RT
76 Houston
6'8 | 320 lbs | exp. 6

Ryan **WENDELL** | RG
62 Fresno State
6'2 | 300 lbs | exp. 6

Tim **WRIGHT** | TE
81 Rutgers
6'4 | 235 lbs | exp. 2

Stephen **GOSTKOWSKI** | K
3 Memphis
6'1 | 215 lbs | exp. 9

Kyle **ARRINGTON** | CB

25 Hofstra
5'10 | 190 lbs | exp. 6

Akeem **AYERS** | LB

55 UCLA
6'3 | 255 lbs | exp. 4

Brandon **BROWNER** | RCB

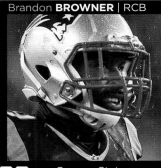

39 Oregon State
6'4 | 221 lbs | exp. 5

Patrick **CHUNG** | S

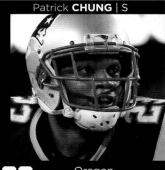

23 Oregon
5'11 | 210 lbs | exp. 6

Jamie **COLLINS** | LB

91 Southern Mississippi
6'3 | 250 lbs | exp. 2

Dont'a **HIGHTOWER** | LB

54 Alabama
6'3 | 270 lbs | exp. 3

Chandler **JONES** | RE

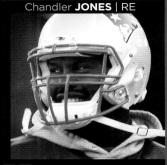

95 Syracuse
6'5 | 265 lbs | exp. 3

Malcolm **BUTLER** | CB

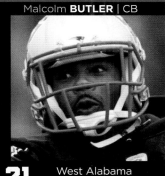

21 West Alabama
5'11 | 190 lbs | exp. R

Devin **McCOURTY** | S

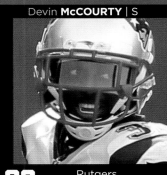

32 Rutgers
5'10 | 195 lbs | exp. 5

Rob **NINKOVICH** | DE

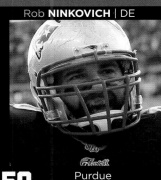

50 Purdue
6'2 | 260 lbs | exp. 9

Darrelle **REVIS** | LCB

24 Pittsburgh
5'11 | 198 lbs | exp. 8

Logan **RYAN** | CB

26 Rutgers
5'11 | 195 lbs | exp. 2

Vince **WILFORK** | DT

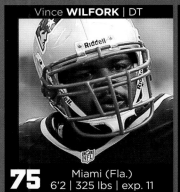

75 Miami (Fla.)
6'2 | 325 lbs | exp. 11

Ryan **ALLEN** | P

6 Louisiana Tech
6'2 | 215 lbs | exp. 2

'I DON'T CARE HOW YOU GOT HERE; IT'S WHAT YOU DO WHEN YOU GET HERE.'
BILL BELICHICK

Bill **BELICHICK** | HEAD COACH

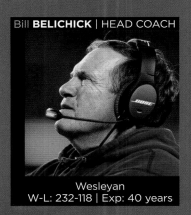

Wesleyan
W-L: 232-118 | Exp: 40 years